AUTOBIOGRAPHY OF
SAMUEL S. HILDEBRAND

AUTOBIOGRAPHY OF SAMUEL S. HILDEBRAND

SAMUEL S. HILDEBRAND,
JAMES W. EVANS,
ABRAHAM WENDELL KEITH

9 789390 215362

ISBN: 978-93-90215-36-2

Published: 1870

LECTOR HOUSE

LECTOR HOUSE LLP
E-MAIL: lectorpublishing@gmail.com

SAM HILDEBRAND DRIVEN FROM HOME.

AUTOBIOGRAPHY OF SAMUEL S. HILDEBRAND,

THE RENOWNED MISSOURI "BUSHWHACKER" AND UNCONQUERABLE ROB ROY OF AMERICA; BEING HIS COMPLETE CONFESSION

RECENTLY MADE TO THE WRITERS, AND CAREFULLY COMPILED

BY

JAMES W. EVANS AND A. WENDELL KEITH, M. D.,

OF ST. FRANCOIS COUNTY, MO.;

TOGETHER WITH ALL THE FACTS CONNECTED WITH HIS EARLY HISTORY.

1870.

PROOF OF AUTHENTICITY.

This is to certify that I, the undersigned, am personally acquainted with Samuel S. Hildebrand (better known as "Sam Hildebrand, the Missouri Bushwhacker," etc.,) and have known him from boyhood; that during the war, and on several occasions since its termination, he promised to give me a full and complete history of his whole war record; that on the night of January 28th, 1870, he came to my house at Big River Mills, in St. Francois county, Missouri, in company with Charles Burks, and gave his consent that I and Charles Burks, in conjunction, might have his confession whenever we were prepared to meet him at a certain place for that purpose; that in the latter part of March, 1870, in the presence of Sam Hildebrand alone, I did write out his confession as he gave it to me, then and there, until the same was completed; and that afterwards James W. Evans and myself, from the material I thus obtained, compiled and completed the said confession, which is now presented to the public as his Autobiography.

A. WENDELL KEITH, M. D.

* * * * *

STATE OF MISSOURI,
County of Ste. Genevieve.

On this, 14th day of June, 1870, before me, Henry Herter, a Notary Public within and for said county, personally appeared W. H. Couzens, J. N. Burks and G. W. Murphy of the above county and State, and on being duly sworn they stated that they were well acquainted with Charles Burks of the aforesaid county, and A. Wendell Keith, M. D., of St. Francois county, Missouri, and to their certain knowledge the facts set forth in the foregoing certificate are true and correct, and that Samuel S. Hildebrand also acknowledged to them afterwards that he had made to them his complete confession.

WM. H. COUZENS, Major C. S. A.,
J. N. BURKS,
G. W. MURPHY.

Subscribed and sworn to before me, this 14th day of June, 1870.

HENRY HERTER,
Notary Public.

* * * * *

The Statement made by A. Wendell Keith, M. D., is entitled to credit from the fact of his well-known veracity and standing in society.

Hon. ELLIS G. EVANS,
Senator, Rolla District.
Hon. E. C. SEBASTIAN,
Representative, St. Francois county.
Hon. MILTON P. CAYCE,
Senator, Rolla District.
FRANKLIN MURPHY,
Senator, Rolla District.
WILLIAM R. TAYLOR,
Senator, Rolla District. Hon.
JOSEPH BOGY,
Senator, Rolla District.
CHARLES ROZIER,
Senator, Rolla District.

* * * * *

EXECUTIVE OFFICE, JEFFERSON CITY, Mo.,
June 22, 1870.

I hereby certify that the persons whose official signatures appear above have been commissioned for the offices indicated; and my personal acquaintance with Dr. Keith, Honorables Evans, Sebastian, Cayce, Bogy and Sheriff Murphy is such that I say without hesitation their statements are entitled to full faith and credit.

J. W. McCLURG,
Governor of Missouri.

PREFACE.

The public having been grossly imposed upon by several spurious productions purporting to be the "Life of Sam Hildebrand," we have no apology to offer for presenting the reader with his authentic narrative.

His confession was faithfully written down from his own lips, as the foregoing certificates abundantly prove.

From this copious manuscript we have prepared his autobiography for the press, with a scrupulous care to give it literally, so far as the arbitrary rules of language would permit. Sam Hildebrand and the authors of this work were raised up from boyhood together, in the same neighborhood, and we are confident that no material facts have been suppressed by Hildebrand in his confession.

The whole narrative is given to the reader without any effort upon our part either to justify or condemn his acts. Our design was to give the genuine autobiography of Sam Hildebrand; this we have done.

The book, as a record of bloody deeds, dare-devil exploits and thrilling adventures, will have no rival in the catalogue of wonders; for it at once unfolds, with minute accuracy, the exploits of Hildebrand, of which one-half had never yet been told. Without this record the world would forever remain in ignorance of the *night history* of his astounding audacity.

We here tender our thanks to those of our friends who have kindly assisted us in this work, prominent among whom is Miss Hilda F. Sharp, of Jefferson City, Mo., who furnished us with those beautiful pencil sketches from which our engravings were made.

JAMES W. EVANS,
A. WENDELL KEITH, M. D.

BIG RIVER MILLS, Mo., June, 1870.

CONTENTS

CONTENTS

LIST OF ILLUSTRATIONS

INTRODUCTION.

THE ORIGIN AND HISTORY OF THE HILDEBRAND FAMILY.

Before proceeding with the Autobiography of Samuel S. Hildebrand, we would call the attention of the reader to the fact, that since notoriety has been thrust upon the subject of these memoirs, public attention has been pointed to the fact, that in German history, the Hildebrands occupy a very prominent position.

The authors of this work, by a diligent research into ancient German literature, have been able to trace the origin and history of the Hildebrand family, with tolerable accuracy, to the beginning of the ninth century. The name Hildebrand or Hildebrandt is as old as the German language. Hilde, in ancient German, signified a "Hero," and brand, a "blaze or flame." It is thought by some writers that the name doubtless signified a "flaming hero."

Whether this is the case or not, it matters but little, as the fact remains clearly defined that the first man of that name known to history was a hero in every sense of the word. The "Heldenbuch" or Book of Heroes, in its original form, dates back to the eighth century. It is a beautiful collection of poems relative to Dietrich or Theodoric. It was written down from memory by the Hessian monks on the outer pages of an old Latin manuscript, and was first published by Eccard in prose, but it was afterwards discovered that the songs were originally in rhyme.

The poem treats of the expulsion of Dietrich of Vaum out of his dominions by Ermenrick, his escape to Attila and his return after an adventurous exile of thirty years. Hildebrand (the old Dietrich) encounters his son, whom he left at home in his flight, in a terrible encounter without knowing who he was. We will present the reader with Das Hildebrands lied (The song of Hildebrand), not on account of any literary merit it may possess, but because of its great antiquity and its popularity among the German people at one time, and by whom it was dramatized.

THE SONG OF HILDEBRAND.

"I must be up and riding," spoke Master Hildebrand,
"'Tis long since I have greeted the distant Berner land;
For many a pleasant summer in foreign lands we've been,
But thirty years have vanished since I my wife have seen."

"Wilt thou be up and riding?" outspoke Duke Amelung;
"Beware! since *one* should meet thee—a rider brave and young.

Right by the Berner market—the brave Sir Alebrand;
If twelve men's strength were in thee, he'd throw thee to the sand!"

"And doth he scorn the country in such a haughty mood?
I'll cleave in twain his buckler—'twill do him little good;
I'll cleave in twain his armor with a resistless blow,
Which for a long year after shall cause his mother woe."

Outspoke of Bern, Sir Dietrich, "now let that counsel be,
And slay him not, old hero, but take advice from me:
Speak gently to the Ritter, a kind word soonest mends;
And let your path be peaceful, so shall ye both be friends!"

And as he reached the garden, right by the mart of Berne;
There came against him riding, a warrior fierce and stern.
A brave young knight in armor, against Sir Hildebrand;
"What seekest thou, old Ritter, in this, thy father's land?"

"Thou bearest splendid armor, like one of royal kind;
So bright thy glit'ering corselet, mine eyes are stricken blind;
Thou, who at home should'st rest thee, and shun a warrior's stroke,
And slumber by the fireside," the old man laughed and spoke.

"Should *I* at firesides rest me, and nurse me well at home,
Full many a fight awaits me, to many a field I'll come.
In many a rattling foray, shall I be known and feared;
Believe my word, thou youngster, 'twas thus I blanched my beard."

"That beard will I tear from thee, though great may be thy pain.
Until the blood-drops trickling, have sprinkled all the plain;
Thy fair green shield and armor, must thou resign to me,
Than seek the town, contented my prisoner to be.

"My armor and my fair green shield have warded many a blow;
I trust that God in Heaven still will guard me from my foe."
No more they spoke together, but grasped their weapons keen,
And what the two most longed for, soon came to pass, I ween!

With glittering sword, the younger struck such a sudden blow,
That with its force the warrior, Sir Hildebrand, bent low;
The youth in haste recoiling, sprang twelve good steps behind,
"Such leaps," exclaimed the gray-beard, "were learned of womankind."

"Had I learned ought of woman, it were to me a shame,
Within my father's castle are many knights of fame;
Full many knights and riders about my father throng,
And what as yet, I know not, I trust to learn ere long."

Sir Hildebrand was cunning, the old gray bearded man,
For when the youth uplifted, beneath his sword he ran;
Around the Ritter's girdle his arms he tightly bound,
And on the ground he cast him—there lies he on the ground!

"Who rubs against the kittles, may spotless keep who can—
How fares it now, young hero, against the *old gray man*?
Now quickly speak and shrive thee, for I thy priest will be;
Say, art thou a young Wolfing? perhaps I'll let thee free."

"Like wolves are all the Wolfing, they ran wild in the wood,
But I'm a Grecian warrior, a rider brave and good;
Frau Ute is my mother, she dwelleth near this spot,
And *Hildebrand*, my father, albeit he knows us not!"

"Is Ute then thy mother, that monarch's daughter free?
Seekest thou thy father, Hildebrand? then know that *I* am he!"
Uplifted he his golden helm, and kissed him on the mouth;
Now God be praised that both are safe! the old man and the youth.

"Oh, father dear, those bloody wounds!" 'twas thus the young knight said:
"Now would I three times rather bear those blows upon my head."
"Be still, be still, my own dear son! the wounds will soon be past;
And God in Heaven above be praised, that we have met at last!"

This lasted from the noonday well to the vesper tide,
Then back into the city Sir Alebrand did ride.
What bears he on his helmet? a little cross of gold;
Who is he that rides beside him? his own dear father old.

And with him to his castle, old Hildebrand he bore,
And with his own hands served him—the mother grieved full sore—
"Ah, son, my ever dearest son, the cause I fain would know,
Why a strange prisoner, like this, should e'er be honored so?"

"Now, silence, dearest mother, and list to what I say!
He almost slew me on the heath in open light to-day;
He ne'er shall wear, good mother, a prisoner's attire,
'Tis Hildebrand, the valient, thy husband and my sire!

Oh, mother, dearest mother, do him all honor now;"
Then flew she to her husband, and served him well, I trow;
What holds the brave old father? a glittering ring of gold;
He drops it in the wine cup—it is her husband old!

We congratulate our readers on having survived the reading of the above poem, written a thousand years ago, about old Dietrich, the "father Abraham" of all the Hildebrands; but he must not forget that he is subject to a relapse, for here are two verses not taken from the "Book of Heroes," but from an old popular song in use to this day among the peasantry in South Germany:

HILDEBRAND AND HIS SON HUDEBRAND.

Hildebrand and his son Hudebrand—Alebrand,
Rode off together with sword in hand—sword in hand—
To make fierce war on Venice;

Hildebrand and his son Hudebrand—Alebrand,
Never could find the Venetian land—'netian land.
With flaming swords to menace!

Hildebrand and his son Hudebrand—Alebrand,
Got drunk as pigs with a jolly band—jolly band,
All the while swearing and bawling;
Hildebrand and his son Hudebrand—Alebrand,
Drank till they could neither walk nor stand—walk nor stand,
Home on all fours they went a crawling.

The reader will perceive that the peasantry are disposed to "poke fun" at the great ancestor of the Hildebrand family; this, however, we will attribute to envy, and make no effort to prove that "Hildebrand and his son Hudebrand" were Good Templars, lest we prove too much, and cause the reader to doubt their Dutch origin altogether.

Following the geneology down, we meet with several of the Hildebrands celebrated in the ecclesiastical, literary and scientific world. Of the parentage of Gregory VII. but little is known more than that he was a Hildebrand, born near Rome, but of German parents. On becoming a Roman Pontiff in 1077, he assumed the name of Gregory. He occupied the chair of St. Peter for eight years, during which time he assumed an authority over the crowned heads of Europe, never before attempted. He was a bold man, but was driven from his chair in 1085.

George Frederick Hildebrand was a famous physician, who was born June 5, 1764, at Hanover. He was one of the most learned men of his age; was appointed professor of Anatomy at Brunswick, but he soon took the chair of Chemistry, at Erlangen, in Bavaria. He died March 23, 1816, leaving some of the most elaborate and valuable works ever written.

Ferdinand Theodore Hildebrand was born Juno 2, 1804, and under the tuition of Professor Schadaw, at Berlin, he became very renowned as a painter. He followed his tutor to Dusseldorf in 1826, and was one of the most celebrated artists of the Academy of Painting at that place. In 1830 Hildebrand visited Italy to view the productions of some of the old masters, and afterwards traveled through the Netherlands. Some of his best pictures were drawn to represent scenes in the works of Shakspeare, of which "King Lear mourning over the death of Cordelia," was perhaps the most important. But among the critics, "The sons of Edward" was considered his greatest production.

It is not our purpose to name all the illustrious Hildebrands who have figured in German history or literature; for it must be borne in mind that from the ninth century down to the sixteenth, the name Hildebrand was almost invariably applied as a given name; it was not until that century that it appears as a sur-name. It is a fact, however, well known to historians, that the same given name is frequently retained in a family, and handed down from one generation to another perhaps for one thousand years.

In the southern part of Germany the name Hildebrand was borne by a certain class of vassals, but in the Northern States of that country, there were families of noble birth by the same name. The record of those nobles runs back with a great deal of certainty to a very remote period of German history—beyond which, the dim out-lines of tradition alone can be our guide. This tradition, whether entitled to credit or not, traces the geneology of the Hildebrands in the line of nobles up to Sir Hildebrand, the exiled hero mentioned in the Book of Heroes.

According to the record of the Hildebrand family, as given by Henry Hildebrand of Jefferson county, Missouri, to the authors of this work; the seventh generation back reaches to Peter Hildebrand of Hanover. He was born in 1655, and was the youngest son of a nobleman. His father having died while Peter was yet a boy, he was educated at a military school, and after arriving to manhood he served several years in the army. Returning at length, he was vexed at the cold reception he received from his elder brother, who now inherited the estate with all the titles of nobility belonging to the family. He resolved to emigrate to the wild solitudes of America, where individual worth and courage was the stepping stone to honor and distinction.

His family consisted of a wife and three children; his oldest son, Jacob, was born in 1680; when he was ten years of age the whole family emigrated to New Amsterdam, remained three years and then settled in the northern part of Pennsylvania, where he died a few years afterwards.

Jacob Hildebrand's second son, Jacob, was born in 1705. He was fond of adventure and joined in several exploring expeditions in one of which he was captured by a band of Miami Indians, and only escaped by plunging into the Ohio river and concealing himself under a drift of floating logs. His feelings of hostility against the Indians prompted him to join the expedition against them under Lieutenant Ward, who erected a fort at what is now called Pittsburg, in 1754, here he was killed in a vain attempt to hold the garrison against the French and Indians under Contrecoeur.

His third son, John Hildebrand, was born in 1733, and at the death of his father was twenty-one years of age. Like most of the frontiermen of this early period, he seemed to have an uncontrolable love of adventure. His most ardent desire was to explore the great valley of the Mississippi. At the period of which we are now speaking (1754), he joined James M. Bride and others and passed down the Ohio river in a canoe; to his regret, however, the company only reached the mouth of the Kentucky river, cut their initials in the barks of trees, and then returned. In 1770 he removed to Missouri. His family consisted of his wife and two boys—Peter was born in 1758, and Jonathan in 1762. He built a flat-boat on the banks of the Ohio, and taking a bountiful supply of provisions, he embarked with his family. To avoid the Indians he kept as far from each shore as possible, and never landed but once to pass around the shoals. On reaching the Mississippi he spent more than a week in ascending that river to gain a proper point for crossing. He landed on the western side at Ste. Genevieve.

Viewing the country there as being rather thickly settled, he moved back into the wilderness about forty miles and settled on Big River at the mouth of Saline creek. He was the first settler in that country which was afterwards organized as

Jefferson county. He opened a fine farm on Saline creek, built houses, and considered himself permanently located in that wild country. The Indians were unfriendly, and their hostility toward white settlers seemed to increase until 1780, when Peter Chouteau, by order of the Lieutenant Governor of Louisiana, went to see Hildebrand and warned him to leave on account of Indian depredations. He then removed to Ste. Genevieve.

In 1783, Peter Hildebrand left Ste. Genevieve and settled on Big River in the same neighborhood where his father had resided. He had a wife and four children, whose names were, Isaac, Abraham, David, and Betsy. He was a good marksman and very fond of hunting. After he had resided there about one year, he was shot and killed by the Indians on the bank of Big River one morning while on his return from hunting wild game; after which the family removed nearer to a settlement.

In 1802, David Hildebrand settled on Big River, and about the same time Jonathan Hildebrand settled himself permanently on the same river. He lived until the commencement of the late war, and then died at the age of one hundred years. He had three sons, whose names are, George, Henry, and Samuel.

In 1832, George Hildebrand and his family moved higher up on Big River and settled in St. Francois county—his house was the Hildebrand homestead referred to in these pages—and he was the father of Samuel S. Hildebrand, whose Autobiography we now submit to our readers.

AUTOBIOGRAPHY OF SAMUEL S. HILDEBRAND.

CHAPTER I.

Introduction. — Yankee Fiction. — Reasons for making a full confession.

Since the close of the late rebellion, knowing that I had taken a very active part during its progress several of my friends have solicited me to have my history written out in full. This anxiety to obtain the history of an individual so humble as myself, may be attributed to the fact, that never perhaps since the world began, have such efforts been put forth by a government for the suppression of one man alone, as have been used for my capture, both during the war and since its termination. The extensive military operations carried on by the Federal government in South-east Missouri, were in a great measure designed for my special destruction.

Since the close of the rebellion, while others are permitted to remain at home in peace, the war, without any abatement whatever, has continued against me with a vindictiveness and a lavish expenditure of money that has no parallel on this continent; but through it all, single-handed, have I come out unscathed and unconquered.

My enemies have thrust notoriety upon me, and have excited the public mind at a distance with a desire to know who I am and what I have done. Taking advantage of this popular inquiry, some enterprising individual in an eastern state has issued two or three novels purporting to be my history, but they are not even founded on fact, and miss the mark about as far as if they were designed for the Life of Queen Victoria. I seriously object to the use of my name in any such a manner. Any writer, of course, who is afflicted with an irresistible desire to write fiction, has a perfect right to do so, but he should select a fictitious name for the hero of his novels, that his works may stand or fall, according to their own intrinsic merit, rather than the name of an individual whose notoriety alone would insure the popularity of his books. But an attempt to palm a novel on the inquiring public as a history of my life, containing as it does a catalogue of criminal acts unknown to me in all my career, is not only a slander upon myself, but a glaring fraud upon the public.

Much of our misfortune as a nation may be attributed to the pernicious influence of the intolerant, intermeddling, irrepressible writers of falsehood. In a community where the spirit of fiction pervades every department of literature and all the social relations of life, writers become so habituated to false coloring and deception, that plain unadorned truth has seldom been known to eminate from their perverted brains; it would be just as impossible for them to write down a naked fact as it would for the Prince of Darkness to write a volume of psalms.

The friend who has finally succeeded in tracing me to my quiet retreat in the wild solitudes of the down trodden South, is requesting me to make public the whole history of my life, without any attempt at palliation, concealment or apology. This I shall now proceed to do, in utter disregard to a perverted public opinion, and without the least desire or expectation of receiving justice from the minds of those who never knew justice, or sympathy from those who are destitute of that ingredient.

The necessity that was forced upon me to act the part I did during the reign of terror in Missouri, is all that I regret. It has deprived me of a happy home and the joys of domestic peace and quietude; it has driven me from the associations of childhood, and all the scenes of early life that so sweetly cling to the memory of man; it has caused my kind and indulgent mother to go down into her grave sorrowing; it has robbed me of three affectionate brothers who were brutally murdered and left weltering in their own innocent blood; it has reduced me and my family to absolute want and suffering, and has left us without a home, and I might almost say, without a country.

A necessity as implacable as the decrees of Fate, was forced upon me by the Union party to espouse the opposite side; and all the horrors of a merciless war were waged unceasingly against me for many months before I attempted to raise my hand in self defense. But fight I must, and fight I did! War was the object, and war it was. I never engage in but one business at a time—my business during the war was killing enemies. It is a very difficult matter to carry on a war for four years without some one getting hurt. If I did kill over a hundred men during the war, it was only because I was in earnest and supposed that everybody else was. My name is cast out as evil because I adopted the military tactics not in use among large armies. They were encumbered with artillery and fought where they had ample room to use it, I had no artillery and generally fought in the woods; my plan was the most successful, for in the regular army the rebels did not kill more than one man each during the war.

CHAPTER II.

Early History of the Hildebrand family.—Settled in St. Francois county, Missouri.—Sam Hildebrand born.—Troublesome Neighbors.—Union Sentiments.

In regard to the early history of the Hildebrand family, I can only state what tradition has handed down from one generation to another. As I have no educa-tion, and can neither read in English nor Dutch, I am not able to give any of the outlines of history bearing upon the origin or acts of the Hildebrands in remote ages. This task I leave for others, with this remark, that tradition connects our family with the Hildebrands who figured in the German history up to the very or-igin of the Dutch language. The branch of the family to which I belong were driv-en from Bavaria into Netherlands two hundred years ago, where they remained about forty years, and then emigrated to Pennsylvania at the first settlement of that portion of America.

They were a hardy race of people and always shunned a city life, or being cooped up in thickly settled districts; they kept on the outskirts of aggressive civi-lization as it pressed the redman still back into the wild solitudes of the West, thus occupying the middle ground or twilight of refinement. Hence they continually breathed the pure, fresh air of our country's morning, trod through the dewy vales of pioneer life, and drank at Freedom's shady fountains among the unclaimed hills.

They were literally a race of backwoodsmen inured to hardship, and delighted in nothing so much as wild adventure and personal danger. They explored the hills rather than the dull pages of history, pursued the wild deer instead of tame literature, and enjoyed their own thoughts rather than the dreamy notions eminat-ing from the feverish brain of philosophy.

In 1832 my father and mother, George and Rebecca Hildebrand, settled in St. Francois county, Missouri, on a stream called Big River, one of the tributaries of the Meramec which empties into the Mississippi about twenty miles below St. Louis.

The bottom lands on Big River are remarkably fertile, and my father was so fortunate as to secure one of the best bodies of land in that county. Timber grew in abundance, both on the hills and in the valleys, consequently it took a great deal of hard labor to open a farm; but after a few years of close attention, father, by the assistance of his boys who were growing up, succeeded in opening a very large one. He built a large stone dwelling house two stories high, and finished it off in beautiful style, besides other buildings—barns, cribs and stables necessary on every well regulated farm.

Father and mother raised a family of ten children, consisting of seven boys and three girls. I was the fifth one in the family, and was born at the old homestead on Big River, St. Francois county, Missouri, on the 6th day of January, 1836.

The facilities for acquiring an education in that neighborhood were very slim indeed, besides I never felt inclined to go to school even when I had a chance; I was too fond of hunting and fishing, or playing around the majestic bluffs that wall in one side or the other of Big River, the whole length of that crooked and very romantic stream. One day's schooling was all that I ever got in my life; that day was sufficient for me, it gave me a distaste to the very sight of a school house. I only learned the names of two letters, one shaped like the gable end of a house roof, and the other shaped like an ox yoke standing on end. At recess in the afternoon the boys got to picking at me while the teacher was gone to dinner, and I had them every one to whip. When the old tyrant came back from dinner and commenced talking saucy, I gave him a good cursing and broke for home. My father very generously gave me my choice, either to go to school or to work on the farm. I gladly accepted the latter, redoubled my energy and always afterwards took particular pains to please my father in all things, because he was so kind as not to compel me to attend school. A threat to send me to school was all the whipping that I ever required to insure obedience; I was more afraid of that than I was of old "Rawhead-and-bloody-bones," or even the old scratch himself.

In 1850, my father died, but I still remained at the homestead, working for the support of my mother and the rest of the family, until I had reached the age of nineteen years, then, on the 30th day of October, 1854, I married Miss Margaret Hampton, the daughter of a highly esteemed citizen of St. Francois county. I built a neat log house, opened a farm for myself, within half a mile of the old homestead, and we went to housekeeping for ourselves.

From the time that my father first settled on Big River, we had an abundance of stock, and especially hogs. The range was always good, and as the uplands and hills constituted an endless forest of oaks, the inexhaustible supply of acorns afforded all the food that our hogs required; they roamed in the woods, and of course, many of them became as wild as deer; the wild ones remained among the hills and increased until they became very numerous. Whenever they were fat enough for pork, we were in the habit of going into the woods with our guns and our dogs and killing as many of them as we could.

A few years after my father had settled there, a colony of Pennsylvania Dutch had established themselves in our neighborhood; they were very numerous and constituted about two-thirds of the population of our township. They soon set up "wild hog claims," declaring that some of their hogs had also run wild; this led to disputes and quarrels, and to some "fist and skull fighting," in which my brothers and myself soon won the reputation of "bullies." Finding that they had no show at this game, they next resorted to the law, and we had many little law suits before our justice of the peace. The Dutch *out swore* us, and we soon found the Hildebrand family branded by them with the very unjust and unpleasant epithet of "hog thieves;" but *we* went in on the *muscle* and still held the woods.

As our part of the country became more thickly settled and new neighbors came in, they in turn were prejudiced against us; and the rising generation seemed to cling to the same idea, that the Hildebrands seemed to love pork a little too well and needed watching. Unfortunately for me, my old neighbors were union men; all my sympathies too, were decidedly for the union. I heard with alarm the mutterings of war in the distance, like the deep tones of thunder beyond the frowning hills. I had never made politics my study; I had no education whatever, and had to rely exclusively on what others told me. Of course I was easily imposed upon by political tricksters, yet from my heart I deplored the necessity of a resort to arms, if such a necessity did exist, and whether it did or not was more than I could divine.

While my union neighbors and enemies were making the necessary preparations for leaving their families in comfortable circumstances before taking up arms in defense of their country, there were a few shrewd southern men around to magnify and distort the grievances of the southern people. In many cases the men whom they obtained had nothing in the world at stake, no useful object in view, no visible means of acquiring an honest livelihood, and were even without a horse to ride. This, however, only afforded them a pretext for practicing what they called "pressing horses," which was done on a large scale. Neither political principles, patriotic motives, nor love of country prompted this abominable system of horse stealing. It was not confined to either party, and it was a remarkable co-incident how invariably the political sentiments of a horse-pressing renegade would differ from the neighbor who happened to have the fastest horses.

CHAPTER III.

Determination to take no part in the War.—Mr. Ringer killed by Rebels.—The cunning device of Allen Roan.—Vigilance Committee organized.—The baseness of Mobocracy.—Attacked by the
Mob.—Escape to Flat Woods.

In the spring of 1861, the war of the Great Rebellion was inaugurated, and during the following summer was carried on in great fury in many places, but I shall only speak of those occurrences which had a particular bearing upon myself.

I called on some good citizens who were not republicans, and whom I knew to be well posted in the current events of the day, to ask them what course it was best for me to pursue during the unnatural struggle. They advised me to stay at home and attend to my own business. This I determined to do, so I paid no further attention to what was going on, put in my crop of corn at the usual season and cultivated it during the summer.

On the 9th day of August the popular excitement in St. Francois county was greatly increased by the killing of Mr. Ringer, a union man, who was shot at his own house for no other cause than his political principles. He was killed, as I afterwards learned, by Allen Roan and Tom Cooper. It should be borne in mind that Roan was a relative of mine with whom I was on friendly terms. I was not implicated in the death of Ringer in any manner, shape, or form, but suspicion rested upon me; the "Hildebrand gang" were branded with the murder.

I could not check Roan in the rash course he was pursuing; but in all sincerity, I determined to follow the advice given me by a certain union friend, who told me to take no part in the cause that would in the end bring disaster upon myself. It was good advice; why then did I not follow it? In the presence of that Being who shall judge the quick and the dead, I shall truthfully and in a few words explain the whole matter. I had no sooner made up my mind fully what course to pursue, than I was caught in a cunningly devised trap that settled my destiny forever.

One evening Allen Roan came to my field where I was plowing and proposed swapping horses with me; the horse which he said he had bought was a better one than my own, so I consented to make the exchange; finding afterwards that the horse would not work in harness, I swapped him off the next day to Mr. Rogers.

Prior to this time my neighbors had organized themselves into what they called a Vigilance Committee, and were moving in squads night and day to put down horse stealing. Only a few of the committee were dangerous men, but Firman McIlvaine, who was put at the head of the gang was influenced by the worst element in the community; it became a political machine for oppression and bloodshed under the guidance of James Craig, John House, Joe McGahan, John Dunwoody, William Patton, and others, who were swearing death to every man implicated in any way with the southern recruits who were pressing horses.

The horse I had traded for from Allen Roan and which Rogers obtained from me, proved to be the property of Dunwoody. I was apprised of the fact by a friend at night, and told also that they had threatened me and my brother Frank with death if they could find us, and notwithstanding our entire innocence in the matter, we were compelled to hide out. We knew that when the law is wrested from the civil authorities by such men as they were, that anything like a trial would not be permitted. We secreted ourselves in the woods, hoping that matters would take a different turn in a short time; each night I was posted in regard to their threats. I would willingly have surrendered myself to the civil authorities with a guarantee of a fair trial; but to fall into the hands of an unscrupulous mob who were acting in violation of law, particularly when law and order was broken up by the heavy tramp of war, was what we were compelled by all means to avoid. We had no alternative but to elude their search.

It is a fact well known, that in the upheaval of popular passion for the overthrow of law and order under any pretext whatever, a nucleus is formed, around which the most vile, the most turbulent, and the most cowardly instinctively fly. Cowardly villains invariably join in with every mob that comes within their reach; personal enmity and spite is frequently their controling motive; the possible opportunity of redressing some supposed grievance without incurring danger to themselves is their incentive for swelling the mob. A person guilty of any particular crime, to avoid suspicion, is always the most clamorous for blood when some one else stands accused of the same offense. In the Vigilance Committee were found the same materials existing in all mobs. No brave man was ever a tyrant, but no coward ever failed to be one when he had the power. They still kept up the search for me and my brother with an energy worthy of a better cause.

It was now October, the nights were cold and we suffered much for the want of blankets and even for food. We were both unaccustomed to sleeping out at night and were chilled by the cold wind that whistled through the trees. After we had thus continued in the woods about three weeks, I concluded to venture in one night to see my family and to get something to eat, and some bed clothes to keep me more comfortable at night.

I had heard no unusual noise in the woods that day, had seen no one pass, nor heard the tramp of horses feet in any direction.

It was about eleven o'clock at night when I got within sight of the house, no light was burning within; I heard no noise of any kind, and believing that all was right I crept up to the house and whispered "Margaret" through a crack. My wife heard me, and recognizing my voice she noiselessly opened the door and let me in. We talked only in whispers, and in a few minutes she placed my supper upon the table. Just as I was going to eat I heard the top rail fall off my yard fence. The noise did not suit me, so I took my gun in one hand, a loaf of corn bread in the other, and instantly stepped out into the yard by a back door.

McIlvaine and his vigilantees were also in the yard, and were approaching the house from all sides in a regular line. In an instant I detected a gap in their ranks and dashed through it. As they commenced firing I dodged behind a molasses mill that fortunately stood in the yard, it caught nine of their bullets and without doubt saved my life. After the first volley I struck for the woods, a distance of about two hundred yards. Though their firing did not cease, I stopped midway to shoot at their flame of fire, but a thought struck me that it would too well indicate my whereabouts in the open field, so I hastened on until I had gained the edge of the woods, and there I sat down to listen at what was going on at the house. I heard Firman McIlvaine's name called several times, and very distinctly heard his replies and knew his voice. This satisfied me beyond all doubt that the marauders were none other than the self-styled Vigilance Committee.

I was fortunate in my escape, and had a deep sense of gratitude to heaven for my miraculous preservation. Though I had not made my condition much better by my visit, yet I gnawed away, at intervals, upon my loaf of corn bread, and tried to reconcile myself as much as possible to the terrible state of affairs then existing. I saw very plainly that my enemies would not permit me to remain in that vicinity; but the idea of being compelled to leave my dear home where I was born and raised, and to strike out into the unknown world with my family without a dollar in my pocket, without anything except one horse and the clothing we had upon our backs, was anything in the world but cheering. However, I had no alternative; to take care of my dependent and suffering family, was the motive uppermost in my mind at all times.

After the mob had apparently left, my wife came out to me in the woods. Our plans were soon formed; after dressing the children, five in number, as quietly and speedily as possible, she brought them to me at a designated point among the hills in the dark forest. She returned to the house alone, and with as little noise as possible saddled up my horse, and after packing him with what bed clothing and provisions she conveniently could, she circled around among the hills and rejoined me at a place I had named in the deep forest about five miles from our once happy home. Daylight soon made its appearance and enabled me to pick out a place of tolerable security.

We remained concealed until the re-appearance of night and then proceeded on our cheerless wandering. In silence we trudged along in the woods as best we could, avoiding the mud and occasional pools of water. I carried my gun on my shoulder and one of the children on my hip; my wife, packing the baby in her arms, walked quietly by my side. I never was before so deeply impressed with the faith, energy and confiding spirit of woman. As the moon would occasionally peep forth from the drifting clouds and strike upon the pale features of my uncomplaining wife, I thought I could detect a look of cheerfulness in her countenance, and more than once I thought I heard a suppressed titter when either of us got tangled up in the brush. When daylight appeared we were on Wolf creek, a few miles south of Farmington; here we stopped in the woods to cook our breakfast and to rest a while. During the day we proceeded on to what is called Flat Woods, eight miles from Farmington, in the southern part of St. Francois county, and about ten miles north from Fredericktown. From Mr. Griffin I obtained the use of a log cabin in a retired locality, and in a few minutes we were duly installed in our new house.

CHAPTER IV.

McIlvaine's Vigilance Mob.—Treachery of Castleman.—Frank Hildebrand hung by the Mob.—Organization of the Mob into a Militia Company.

The Vigilance Committee, with Firman McIlvaine at its head, was formed ostensibly for the mutual protection against plunderers; yet some bad men were in it. By their influence it became a machine of oppression, a shield for cowards, and the headquarters for tyranny.

After I left Big River my brother Frank continued to conceal himself in the woods until about the middle of November; the weather now grew so cold that he could stand it no longer; he took the advice of Franklin Murphy and made his way to Potosi, and in order to silence all suspicion in regard to his loyalty, he went to Captain Castleman and offered to join the Home Guards. Castleman being intimate with Firman McIlvaine, detained Frank until he had time to send McIlvaine word, and then basely betrayed him into the merciless hands of the vigilant mob.

In order to obtain a shadow of legality for his proceedings, McIlvaine took brother Frank before Franklin Murphy, who at that time was justice of the peace on Big River. Frank was anxious that the justice might try the case; but when Murphy told them that all the authority he had would only enable him to commit him to jail for trial in the proper court, even if the charges were sustained, they were dissatisfied at this, and in order to take the matter out of the hands of the justice and make it beyond his jurisdiction, they declared that he had stolen a horse in Ste. Genevieve county.

The mob then took Frank to Punjaub, in that county, before Justice R. M. Cole, who told them that he was a sworn officer of the law, and that if they should produce sufficient evidence against their prisoner, he could only commit him to jail. This of course did not satisfy the mob; to take the case out of his hands, they stated that the offense he had committed was that of stealing a mule in Jefferson county. They stated also that Frank and Sam Anderson had gone in the night to the house of a Mr. Carney to steal his mare; that Mrs. Carney on hearing them at the gate, went out and told them that Mr. Carney was absent and had rode the mare; that they then compelled Mrs. Carney to go with them a quarter of a mile in her night clothes to show them where Mr. Becket lived; and finally that they went there and stole his horse. Failing however to obtain the co-operation of the Justice in carrying out their lawless designs, the mob left with their prisoner, declaring that they were going to take him to Jefferson county for trial.

FRANK HILDEBRAND HUNG BY THE MOB.

The sad termination of the affair is soon told. The mob took my kind, inoffensive brother about five miles and hung him without any trial whatever, after which they threw his body in a sink-hole thirty feet in depth, and there his body laid for more than a month before it was found. A few weeks after this cold blooded murder took place, Firman McIlvaine had the audacity to boast of the deed, declaring positively that Frank had been hung by his express orders. This murder took place on the 20th day of November, 1861, about a month after I had been driven from Big River.

A few nights after my arrival at Flat Woods I made my way back to my old home in order to bring away some more of my property, but on arriving there I found that my house had been robbed and all my property either taken away or destroyed. I soon learned from a friend that the Vigilance Committee had wantonly destroyed everything that they did not want. I returned to Flat Woods in a very despondent mood. I was completely broken up.

The union men were making war upon me, but I was making no war upon them, for I still wished to take no part in the national struggle. I considered it "a rich man's war and a poor man's fight." But a sense of my wrongs bore heavily upon me; I had been reduced to absolute poverty (to say nothing of the murder of my brother) by the unrelenting cruelty of Firman McIlvaine who was a rich man, drowned in luxury and surrounded by all the comforts of life that the eye could wish, or a cultivated appetite could desire.

The war was now raging with great fury in many sections of the country; yet I remained at home intent on making a living for my family, provided I could do so without being molested, but during all the time I was at work, I had to keep a sharp lookout for my enemies.

That leprous plague spot—the Vigilance Committee—finally ripened and culminated in the formation of a company of militia on Big River, with James Craig for Captain and Joe McGahan for First Lieutenant. The very act for which they were so anxious to punish others, on mere suspicion, they themselves now committed with a high hand.

They were ordered to disarm southern sympathizers and to seize on articles contraband of war, such as arms and ammunition. This gave them great latitude; the cry of "disloyal" could be very easily raised against any man who happened to have a superabundance of property. "Arms" was construed also to include *arm chairs* and their *arms full* of everything they could get their hands on; "guns" included *Gunn's Domestic Medicine;* a fine claybank mare was confiscated because she looked so *fiery,* and a spotted mule because it had so many *colors;* they took a gun from Mr. Metts merely because he lived on the *south side* of Big River; they dipped heavily into the estate of Dick Poston, deceased, by killing the cattle for beef and dividing it among themselves, under the pretext that if Dick Poston had been living, he most undoubtedly would have been a rebel.

CHAPTER V.

His house at Flat Woods attacked by Eighty Soldiers.—Wounded.—
Miraculous Escape.—Captain Bolin.—Arrival in Green County,
Arkansas.

In April, 1862, after we had lived at Flat Woods during six months of perfect tranquility, that same irrepressible Vigilance Committee, or some men who had composed it, learned finally that I was living at Flat Woods. Firman McIlvaine and Joe McGahan succeeded in getting eighty soldiers from Ironton to aid in my capture. I had been hauling wood; as soon as I unloaded the wagon I stepped into the house, and the first thing I knew, the eighty soldiers and the vigilantees were within gunshot and coming under full charge. I seized my gun and dashed through a gap in their lines that Heaven had again left open for my escape. They commenced firing upon me as soon as I was out of the house. The brush being very thick not far off, I saw that my only chance was to gain the woods, and that as soon as possible. I ran through the garden and jumped over a picket fence—this stopped the cavalry for a moment. I made through the brush; but out of the hundreds of bullets sent after me, one struck my leg below the knee and broke a bone. I held up by the bushes as well as I could, to keep them from knowing that I was wounded. While they had to stop to throw down a fence, I scrambled along about two hundred yards further, and crouched in a gully that happened to be half full of leaves; I quickly buried myself completely from sight. The soldiers were all around in a short time and scoured the woods in every direction; then they went back and burned the house and everything we had, after which they left and I saw them no more.

Sixteen of Captain Bolin's men on the day before had been seen to cross the gravel road; this, probably, was why the federal soldiers did not remain longer. Captain Bolin was a brave rebel officer, whose headquarters were in Green county, Arkansas, and under whose command some of the most daring spirits who figured in the war, were led on to deeds of heroism scarcely ever equaled.

Our condition was truly deplorable; there I lay in the gully covered up with leaves, with one leg rendered useless, without even the consolation of being allowed to groan; my family, too, were again without shelter; the soldiers had burned everything—clothes, bedding and provisions.

As I lay in that gully, suffering with my wounds inflicted by United States soldiers, I declared war. I determined to fight it out with them, and by the assistance of my faithful gun, "Kill-devil," to destroy as many of my blood-thirsty enemies as I possibly could. To submit to further wrong from their hands would be an insult to the Being who gave me the power of resistance.

After the soldiers had left, my wife came in search of me, believing that I was wounded from the manner in which I seemed to run. I told her to go back, that I was not hurt very bad, and that when she was satisfied that no one was watching around, to come at night and dress my leg. She went, however, in search of some friend on whom we could rely for assistance. Fortunately she came across Mr. Pigg, to whom she related the whole circumstance, and he came immediately to my relief. He was a man of the right stripe; regardless of consequences, he did everything in his power to relieve my suffering, and to supply my family with bedding and provisions. He removed us by night to a place of safety, and liberally gave us all we needed. While I thus lay nursing my wound, my place of concealment was known only to a few men whom we could easily trust.

In my hours of loneliness I had much time for reflection. The terrible strait in which I found myself, naturally led me to the mental inquiry: "Have I the brand of Cain, that the hands of men should be turned against me? What have I done to merit the persecution so cruel and so persistent?" I could not solve the questions; in the sight of a just God I felt that I did not merit such treatment. Sometimes I half resolved to go into some other State on purpose to avoid the war; but I was constantly warned by my friends who were southern men, (the only men with whom I could hold communication at present,) that it would be unsafe to think of doing so, and that my only safety lay in my flight to the southern army. The vigilance mob had nearly destroyed every vestige of sympathy or good feeling I had for the union people. They had reported me, both to the civil and military authorities, as being a horse thief, and, withal, a very dangerous man.

On thinking the matter over I lost all hope of ever being able to reinstate myself in their favor and being permitted to enjoy the peaceful privileges of a quiet citizen. The die was cast—for the sake of revenge, I pronounced myself a Rebel.

I remained very quietly at my place of concealment while my wife doctored my wounded leg for a week before my friend had an opportunity of sending word to any of Captain Bolin's men to come to my relief. As soon as my case was made known to them, however, a man was dispatched to see me for the purpose of learning all the particulars in the case. He came and asked me a great many questions, but answered none. When he arose to depart he only said, "all right—rest easy."

The next night I was placed in a light spring wagon among some boxes of drugs and medicines, and was told that my wife and family would be taken to Bloomfield by Captain Bolin in a short time, and protected until I could come after them. A guard of two men accompanied us, and rode the whole night without speaking a word to any one. Nearly the whole route was through the woods, and although the driver was very watchful and used every precaution against making a noise, yet in the darkness of the night I was tumbled about among the boxes pretty roughly.

When daylight came we halted in a desolate looking country, inhabited only by wild animals of the forest. We had traveled down on the western side of St. Francois river, and were now camped near the most western bend on that river near the southern line of Madison county; we remained all day at that point, and I spent most of my time in sleeping. When the sun had dipped behind the western hills we again commenced our journey. Our course seemed to bear more to the eastward than it did the night before, and as we were then in a country not so badly infested with Federals, we traveled a good part of our time in narrow, crooked roads, but they were rough beyond all description, and I was extremely glad when about eight o'clock in the morning we halted for breakfast on the western bank of St. Francois river, about midway between Bloomfield, in Stoddard county, and Crane creek, in Butler.

While resting here a scouting party from General Jeff. Thompson's camp came riding up.

"Well boys! what have you in your wagon?"

"Drugs and medicines for Captain Bolin's camp."

On hearing this they dismounted and kept up a lively conversation around the camp fire. Among their number was a jovial fellow who kept the rest all laughing. I thought I knew the voice, and as I turned over to peep through a hole in the wagon bed, he heard me and sprang to his feet.

"Who in thunderation have you in the wagon?"

"Some fellow from St. Francois county, wounded and driven off by the Federals."

"The devil! why that is my native county. I'll take a look at that fellow. It's Sam Hildebrand as I live! How do you do, old rapscallion?"

"Well, well, if I haven't run across Tom Haile, the dare-devil of the swamps!"

"Old 'drugs and medicines' what are you doing here? trying to pass yourself off for a great medicinal root I suppose. Do you feel tolerable better? I'm afraid you are poison. Say, Sam, did you bring some good horses down with you?"

"Hush Tom! if they find out that I'm not a horse thief, they will drum me out of camp!"

The party soon prepared to start; the first man who attempted to mount came near being dashed to the ground in consequence of the rattling of a tin cup some one had tied to his spur. Tom said it was a perfect shame to treat any man in that way; the man seemed to think so, too, judging from the glance he cast at Tom. But they mounted, dashed through a sheet of muddy water, then over a rocky point, and soon were far away amid the dim blue hills.

We started on, and after traveling until about midnight, we reached the State line between Missouri and Arkansas, there we remained until morning; on starting again we were in Green county, Arkansas, and sometime during the day we arrived safely at the Headquarters of Captain Bolin, and I was welcomely received into the little community of families, who were here assembled for mutual protection—most of them were the families of Captain Bolin's men. I received every attention from them that my necessities required, and as my wound seemed to be doing well, I felt for a time quite at home.

CHAPTER VI.

Interview with Gen. Jeff. Thompson.—Receives a Major's Commission.—Interview with Captain Bolin.—Joins the "Bushwhacking
Department."

Captain Bolin with most of his forces were somewhere in the vicinity of
Bloomfield, Missouri, and as I was anxious to identify myself with the army, I got
the use of a horse as soon as I was able to ride, and in company with several others
proceeded across the swampy country east of the St. Francis river, for the purpose
of joining General Jeff. Thompson. I reached his headquarters in safety, and stayed
about camp, frequently meeting acquaintances from Missouri and occasionally
getting news from home. As soon as I could gain admission to the General's headquarters I did so, and he received me very kindly. He listened very attentively to
me as I proceeded to state my case to him—how my brother had been murdered,
how I had barely escaped the same fate, and how I had finally been driven from
the country.

General Thompson reflected a few moments, then seizing a pen he rapidly
wrote off a few lines and handing it to me he said, "here, I give you a Major's commission; go where you please, take what men you can pick up, fight on your own
hook, and report to me every six months." I took the paper and crammed it down
into my pantaloon's pocket and walked out. I could not read my commission, but I
was determined to ask no one to read it for me, for that would be rather degrading
to my new honor.

I retired a little distance from camp and taking my seat on an old cypress log,
I reflected how the name of "Major Sam Hildebrand" would look in history. I did
not feel comfortable over the new and very unexpected position in which I had
been placed. I knew nothing of military tactics; I was not certain whether a Major
held command over a General or whether he was merely a bottle washer under a
Captain. I determined that if the latter was the case, that I would return to Green
county and serve under Captain Bolin.

As I had no money with which to buy shoulder-straps, I determined to fight
without them. I was rather scarce of money just at that time; if steamboats were
selling at a dollar a piece, I did not have money enough to buy a canoe paddle.
I stayed in camp, however, several days taking lessons, and hearing the tales of
blood and pillage from the scouts as they came in from various directions.

By this time my wound felt somewhat easier, so I mounted my horse and
made my way back to Green county, and arrived safely at Captain Bolin's head-

quarters. The Captain was at home, and I immediately presented myself before him. He said he had heard of me from one of his scouts, and was highly gratified that one of his men had seen proper to have me conveyed to his headquarters.

"I presume," said he, "that you have been to the headquarters of General Jeff. Thompson. Did you see the 'Old Swamp Fox?'"

"I did."

"What did he do for you?"

Here I pulled my commission from my pocket, that now looked more like a piece of gunwadding than anything else, and handed it to the Captain.

"Well, Major Hildebrand—"

"Sam, if you please."

"Very well then, what do you propose to do?"

"I propose to fight."

"But Major—"

"Sam, if you please."

"All right, sir! Sam, I see that you have the commission of a Major."

"Well Captain, I can explain that matter: he formed me into an independent company of my own—to pick up a few men if can get them—go where I please—when I please—and when I go against my old personal enemies up in Missouri, I am expected to do a *Major* part of the fighting myself."

At this the Captain laughed heartily, and after rummaging the contents of an old box he drew forth something that looked to me very much like a bottle. After this ceremony was over he remarked:

"Well sir, the commission I obtained is of the same kind. I have one hundred and twenty-five men, and we are what is denominated 'Bushwhackers'; we carry on a war against our enemies by shooting them; my men are from various sections of the country, and each one perhaps has some grievance to redress at home; in order to enable him to do this effectually we give him all the aid that he may require; after he sets things to right in his section of country, he promptly comes back to help the others in return; we thus swap work like the farmers usually do in harvest time. If you wish an interest in this joint stock mode of fighting you can unite your destiny with ours, and be entitled to all our privileges."

Captain Bolin's proposition was precisely what I so ardently desired. Of the real merits of this war I knew but little and cared still less. To belong to a large army and be under strict military discipline, was not pleasing to my mind; to be brought up in a strong column numbering several thousands, and to be hurled in regular order against a mass of men covering three or four miles square, against whom I had no personal spite, would not satisfy my spirit of revenge. Even in a fierce battle fought between two large opposing armies, not more than one man out of ten can succeed in killing his man; in a battle of that kind he would have no more weight than a gnat on a bull's horn.

I was fully satisfied that the "Bushwhacking department" was the place for me, with the continent for a battle field and the everlasting woods for my headquarters.

CHAPTER VII.

Trip to Missouri.—Kills George Cornecious for reporting on him.—
Kills Firman McIlvaine.—Attempt to kill McGahan and House.—
Returns to Arkansas.

My wound kept me at headquarters for about six weeks after my arrival in Arkansas. During all this time I could not hear a word from my family, for the Federals had possession of every town in that section of country, together with all the roads leading from one county to another.

On the 1st day of June, 1862, having been furnished a horse, I took my faithful gun, "Kill-devil," and started on my first trip back to Missouri. As my success would depend altogether on the secrecy of my movements, I went alone. I traveled altogether in the night, and most of the time through the woods. From Captain Bolin's men I had learned the names of Southern sympathizers along the whole route, so I made it convenient to travel slowly in order to favor my wounds and to get acquainted with our friends.

I arrived in the vicinity of Flat Woods, in St. Francois county, Missouri, on the 12th day of June, and immediately commenced searching for George Cornecious, the man who reported my whereabouts to McIlvaine and the soldiers, thereby causing me to be wounded and expelled from Flat Woods. After searching two days and two nights I succeeded in shooting him; he was the first man I ever killed; a little notch cut in the stock of my gun was made to commemorate the deed.

To avoid implicating my family in any way with my transactions, I satisfied myself with exchanging words with my wife through a friend who was thought by his neighbors to be a Union man. My family resided in a little cabin on Back creek, and my wife was cultivating a garden.

To carry out the darling object I had in view—that of killing Firman McIlvaine—I went to Flat river, and after remaining several days, I took a pone of bread for my rations and walked to his farm on Big river after night.

I passed through his fields, but finding no place where harvesting was going on, I crossed Big river on a fish-trap dam and ranged over the Baker farm on the opposite side of the river, about a mile above Big river Mills, where the McIlvaine family now resided.

I found where harvesting had just commenced in a field which formed the southwestern corner of the farm. This field is on the top of a perpendicular bluff, about one hundred feet high, and is detached from the main farm by a road leading from Ste. Genevieve to Potosi.

A portion of the grain had already been cut on the western side of the field, near the woods; there I took my station in the fence corner, early in the morning, thinking that McIlvaine would probably shock the grain while the negroes were cradling. In this I was mistaken, for I saw him swinging his cradle in another part of the field, beyond the range of my gun.

I next attempted to crawl along the edge of the bluff among the stunted cedars, but had to abandon the attempt because the negroes stopped in the shade of the cedars every time they came around. Then I went back into the woods, and passed down under the bluff, along the edge of the river, until I got opposite the place where they were at work; but I found no place where I could ascend the high rock. I went around the lower end of the bluff, and crawled up to the field on the other side, but I was at too great a distance to get a shot. Finally, I went down to the river and was resting myself near a large flat rock that projected out into the river, where some persons had recently been fishing, when suddenly Firman McIlvaine rode down to the river and watered his horse at a ford about sixty yards below me. I tried to draw a bead on him, but the limb of a tree prevented me, and when he started back he rode too fast for my purpose.

At night I crept under a projecting rock and slept soundly; but very early in the morning I ascended the bluff and secreted myself at a convenient distance from where they had left off cradling. But I was again doomed to disappointment, for, as the negroes were cradling, McIlvaine was shocking the grain in another part of the field.

In the evening, as soon as they had finished cutting the grain, all hands left, and I did not know where they were. I next stationed myself at a short distance from the river, and watched for him to water his horse; but his father presently passed along leading the horse to water.

I again slept under the overhanging rock; and on the next morning (June 23d) I crossed the river on the fish dam, and went to the lower part of McIlvaine's farm. There I found the negroes cutting down a field of rye. They cut away for several hours, until they got it all down within one hundred yards of the fence, before McIlvaine made his first round. On getting a little past me, he stopped to whet his scythe; as soon as he had done so he lowered the cradle to the ground, and for a moment stood resting on the handle.

I fired, and he fell dead.

Nothing but a series of wrongs long continued could ever have induced me to take the life of that highly accomplished young man.

After the outbreak of the war, while others were losing horses, a fine mare was stolen from him. The theft was not committed by me, but my personal enemies probably succeeded in making him believe that I had committed the act.

He was goaded on by evil advisers to take the law into his own hands; my brother Frank was hung without a trial, and his body thrown into a sink-hole, to moulder like that of a beast; my own life had been sought time and again; my wife and tender family were forced to pass through hardships and suffering seldom witnessed in the annals of history. The mangled features of my poor brother; the pale face of my confiding wife; the tearful eyes of my fond children—all would seem to turn reprovingly upon me in my midnight dreams, as if demanding retributive justice. My revenge was reluctant and long delayed, but it came at last.

SAM HILDEBRAND KILLING MCILVAINE.

I remained in the woods, near the residence of a friend for a day or two, and then I concluded to silence Joe McGahan and John House before returning to Arkansas. I proceeded to the residence of the former, who had been very officious in the Vigilance mob, and posted myself in some woods in the field within one hundred yards of the house, just as daylight began to appear. I kept a vigilant watch for him all day, but he did not make his appearance until it had commenced getting dark; then he rode up and went immediately into his house. By this time it was too dark for me to shoot at such a distance. I moved to the garden fence, and in a few minutes he made his appearance in the door with a little child in his arms. The fence prevented me from shooting him below the child, and I could not shoot him in the breast for fear of killing it.

He remained in the door only a minute or two, and then retired into the house; and while I was thinking the matter over, without noticing closely for his reappearance, I presently discovered him riding off. I went to a thicket in his field and slept until nearly day, when I again took my position near the house, and watched until night again set in, but fortunately for him he did not make his appearance.

I now went about four miles to the residence of John House, selected a suitable place for my camp, and slept soundly until daybreak. I watched closely all day, but saw nothing of my enemy. As soon as it was dark I went back to Flat river, and on the next night I mounted my horse and started back to Green county, Arkansas, without being discovered by any one except by those friends whom I called on for provisions.

CHAPTER VIII.

Vigilance mob drives his mother from home.—Three companies of
troops sent to Big river.—Captain Flanche murders Washington Hildebrand and Landusky.—Captain Esroger murders John
Roan.—Capt. Adolph burns the Hildebrand homestead and murders Henry Hildebrand.

I shall now give a brief account of the fresh enormities committed against the
Hildebrand family. The same vindictive policy inaugurated by the Vigilance mob
was still pursued by them until they succeeded, by misrepresentation, in obtaining the assistance of the State and Federal troops for the accomplishment of their
designs.

A Dutch company, stationed at North Big River Bridge, under Capt. Esroger;
a Dutch company stationed at Cadet, under Capt. Adolph, and a French company
stationed at the Iron Mountain, under Capt. Flanche, were all sent to Big River to
crush out the Hildebrand family.

Emboldened by their success in obtaining troops, the Vigilance mob marched
boldly up to the Hildebrand homestead and notified my mother, whom they
found reading her Bible, that she must immediately leave the county, for it was
their intention to burn her house and destroy all her property.

My mother was a true Christian; she was kind and affectionate to everybody;
her hand was always ready to relieve the distressed, and smooth the pillow for the
afflicted; the last sight seen upon earth by eyes swimming in death has often been
the pitying face of my mother, as she hovered over the bed of sickness.

I appeal to all her neighbors—I appeal to everybody who knew her—to say
whether my mother ever had a superior in this respect.

When ordered to leave her cherished home, to leave the house built by her
departed husband, to leave the quiet homestead where she had brought up a large
family, and where every object was rendered dear by a thousand sweet associations that clung to her memory, she turned her mind inwardly, but found nothing
there to reproach her; then to her God she silently committed herself.

She hastily took her Bible and one bed from the house—but nothing more. She
had arrangements made to have her bed taken to the house of her brother, Harvey
McKee, living on Dry Creek, in Jefferson county, distant about thirty five miles.
Then, taking her family Bible in her arms, she burst into a flood of tears, walked
slowly out of the little gate, and left her home forever!

I will here state that I was the only one of the Hildebrand family who espoused the Rebel cause. After the murder of my brother Frank, I had but three brothers left: William, Washington and Henry. William joined the Union army and fought until the close of the war. Washington took no part in the war, neither directly nor indirectly. Never, perhaps, was there a more peaceable, quiet and law-abiding citizen than he was; he never spoke a word that could be construed into a sympathy for the Southern cause, and I defy any man to produce the least evidence against his loyalty, either in word or act. While the war was raging, he paid no attention to it whatever, but was busily engaged in lead mining in the St. Joseph Lead Mines, three miles from Big River Mills, and about six miles from the old homestead. In partnership with him was a young man by the name of Landusky, a kind, industrious, inoffensive man, whose loyalty had never once been doubted. My sister Mary was his affianced bride, but her death prevented the marriage.

My brother Henry was a mere boy, only thirteen years of age. Of course he was too young to have any political principles; he was never accused of being a Rebel; no accusation of any kind had ever been made against him; he was peaceable and quiet, and, like a good boy, he was living with his mother, and doing the best he could toward supporting her. True, he was very young to have the charge of such a farm, but he was a remarkable boy. Turning a deaf ear to all the rumors and excitements around him, he industriously applied himself to the accomplishment of one object, that of taking care of his mother.

On the 6th day of July, 1862, while my brother Washington and Mr. Landusky were working in a drift underground, Capt. Flanche and his company of cavalry called a halt at the mine, and ordered them to come up; which they did immediately.

No questions were asked them, and no explanations were given. Flanche merely ordered them to walk off a few steps toward a tree, which they did; he then gave the word "fire!" and the whole company fired at them, literally tearing them to pieces!

I would ask the enlightened world if there ever was committed a more diabolical deed? If, in all the annals of cruelty, or in the world's wide history, a murder more cold-blooded and cruel could be found?

A citizen who happened to be present ventured to ask in astonishment why this was done; to which Flanche merely replied, as he rode off, "they bees the friends of Sam Hildebrass!"

It was now Capt. Esroger's time to commit some deed of atrocity, to place himself on an equality with Capt. Flanche; so after a moment's reflection, he concluded that the murder of my uncle, John Roan, would be sufficient to place his brutality beyond all question.

John Roan was a man about fifty years of age, was proverbial for his honesty, always paid his debts, and kept himself entirely aloof from either side during the war, but against his loyalty nothing had ever been produced, or even attempted.

One of his sons was in the Union army, and another was a Rebel.

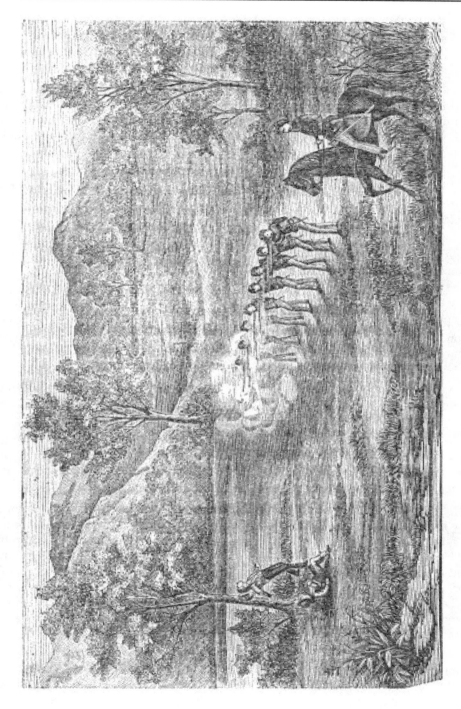

THE MURDER OF WASH. HILDEBRAND AND LANDUSKY.

Being my uncle, and the father of Allen Roan, however, was a sufficient pretext for the display of military brutality.

His house was situated about three miles from St. Joseph Lead Mines and about the same distance from the Hildebrand estate.

On the 10th day of July, Capt. Esroger and his company rode up to his house, and the old man came out onto the porch, with his white locks streaming in the wind, but never once did he dream of treachery. Esroger told him that he "vos one tam prisoner," and detailed six men to guard him and to march along slowly until they should get behind.

They did so until they got about a mile from his house; there they made him step off six paces, and while his eyes were turned towards Heaven, and his hands were slightly raised in the attitude of prayer, the fatal word "fire" was given, and he fell to the earth a mangled corpse.

There was still another actor in this bloody tragedy, who had to tax his ingenuity to the utmost to select a part in which to out do, if possible, the acts of atrocity committed by the others. This was Capt. Adolph.

On the 23rd day of July, Capt. Adolph and his company with an intermixture of the Vigilance mob, went to my mother's house—the Hildebrand homestead—for the purpose of burning it up. The house was two stories high, built of nice cut stone, and well finished within, making it altogether one of the best houses in the county.

The soldiers proceeded to break down the picket fence, and to pitch it into the house for kindling. They refused to let anything be taken out of the house, being determined to burn up the furniture, clothing, bedding, provisions, and everything else connected with it.

All things being now ready, the house was set on fire within, and the flames spread rapidly from room to room, then through the upper floor, and finally out through the roof. The house, with all the outer building was soon wrapped in a sheet of fire.

My little brother Henry and an orphan boy about fourteen years of age, whom my mother had hired to assist Henry in cultivating the farm, were present at the conflagration and stood looking on in mute astonishment. Esroger ordered brother Henry to leave, but whether he knew it was their intention to shoot him after getting him a short distance from the house, as was their custom, it is impossible for me to say. Probably feeling an inward consciousness of never having committed an act to which they could take exceptions, he did not think that they would persist in making him go; so he remained and silently gazed at the burning house, which was the only home he had ever known.

When ordered again to leave, he seemed to be stupefied with wonder at the enormity of the scene before him. Franklin Murphy being present told him it was best to leave; so he mounted his horse and started, but before he got two hundred yards from the house, he was shot and he dropped dead from the horse. Thus perished the poor innocent boy, who could not be induced to believe that the men were base enough to kill him, innocent and inoffensive as he was. But alas! how greatly was he mistaken in them!

They next burned the large frame barn, also the different cribs and stables on the premises; then taking the orphan boy as a prisoner they left.

Some neighbors, a few days afterwards found the body of my little brother and buried him.

This was the crowning act of Federal barbarity toward me and the Hildebrand family, instigated by the low cunning of the infamous Vigilance mob.

I make no apology to mankind for my acts of retaliation; I make no whining appeal to the world for sympathy. I sought revenge and I found it; the key of hell was not suffered to rust in the lock while I was on the war path.

I pity the poor miserable, sniveling creature who would tamely have submitted to it all.

Such a man would be so low in the scale of human conception; so far beneath the lowest grade of humanity, that the head even of an Indian would grow dizzy in looking down upon him.

CHAPTER IX.

Trip with Burlap and Cato. — Killed a Spy near Bloomfield. — Visits his
Mother on Dry Creek. — Interview with his Uncle. — Sees the burning of the homestead at a distance.

As yet, I had heard nothing about the atrocities committed against the remaining members of the Hildebrand family; but in order to stir up my old enemies in
that quarter, I selected two good men, John Burlap and James Cato, to accompany
me in another excursion to St. Francois county, Missouri.

They, too, had been badly treated at the outbreak of the war, and had several
grievances to redress, for which purpose I promised them my future aid. We procured Federal uniforms, and started late in the afternoon of July 13th, 1862; but on
arriving at St. Francis river, we found it out of its banks from the heavy rains that
had fallen the day previous.

My comrades were rather reluctant about venturing into the turbid stream
amid the floating driftwood; but I had ever been impressed with the truth of the
old adage, that it was "bad luck to turn back." I plunged my horse into the stream
and made the opposite shore without much difficulty. I was followed by Burlap
and Cato, who got across safely, but were somewhat scratched by the driftwood.
We built a fire, dried our clothes, took a "snort" from our black bottle, and camped
until morning.

Nothing of interest occurred until we reached the vicinity of Bloomfield, in
Stoddard county, Missouri, when we met a man in citizen's dress, whom we accosted in a very familiar manner, asking him if there were any Rebels in that vicinity. He stated that there was a party of Rebels in Bloomfield, and that we had better
make our way back to Greenville to the command, otherwise we would be sure
to fall into their hands. He stated that he had been with them all day, pretending
that he wanted to enlist; that he had learned all about their plans, and thought
that about to-morrow night they would all be taken in. I inquired if they had not
suspicioned him as a spy? He answered that they had not; that he had completely
deceived them. I then asked him if he did not want to ride behind me and my companions, by turns, until we reached Greenville? He signified his assent by spring-
ing up behind me. I let him ride about two miles, but not exactly in the direction
of Greenville, for I told him that I was aiming to strike a certain cross road, which
seemed to satisfy his mind. He had much to tell us about his exploits as a spy, and
that he had learned the names of all the Rebels in Greenville and Fredericktown.
By this time we had enough. I told him I was Sam Hildebrand, knocked him off
my horse, and then shot him.

I felt no compunction of conscience for having ended the days of such a scoundrel. A little notch underneath the stock of old "Kill-devil" was made, to indicate the probability that he would fail to report.

On the rest of our trip we traveled altogether in the night, and avoided the commission of any act that would be likely to create a disturbance. We arrived safely at the house of my brother-in-law, on Flat river, who lives within ten miles of the Hildebrand homestead.

Here, for the first time, I heard of the murder of my brother Washington, also that of my uncle, John Roan. Mother's house had not yet been burned, but she had been peremptorily driven from it, and had sought refuge with her brother, in Jefferson county. The country was full of soldiers, and the Vigilance mob were in their glory. Their deeds would blacken the name of John A. Murrel, the great land pirate of America, for he never robbed a lady, nor took the bread from orphan children; while they unblushingly did both.

On learning these particulars, I determined to go to Dry Creek for the purpose of seeing my mother, although the soldiers were scouring the country in every direction for fifty miles for my destruction. We started at night, but having to travel a circuitous route, daylight overtook us when within six miles of my uncle's. We made a circuit, as was my custom, around a hillside, and then camped in such a position that we would be close to our pursuers for half an hour before they could find us.

My companions took a nap while I kept watch. They had not been asleep long before I discovered a party of men winding their way slowly in the semi-circle we had made. There were ten of them, all dressed in Federal uniform. I awakened my companions, and they took a peep at them as they were slowly tracking us, at a distance of three hundred yards. We could hardly refrain from making war upon them, the chances being so good for game and a little fun, but my object was to see my mother; so we let them pass on to the place where our tracks would lead them out of sight for a few minutes, then we mounted our horses and rode on to another ridge, making a circuit as before, and camping within a quarter of a mile of our first ambush. On coming to that place, the Federals struck off in another direction, probably finding our tracks a little too fresh for their safety.

When night came, we made our way cautiously through the woods to within a few hundred yards of my uncle's house. I dismounted, and leaving my horse with my comrades, approached the house carefully, and climbed upon a bee-gum to peep through the window. I discovered that there were two strange men in the room, and I thought I got a glimpse of another man around in a corner; but as I leaned a little to one side to get a better view, my bee-gum tilted over, and I fell with a desperate crash on a pile of clapboards. I got up in somewhat of a hurry, and, at about three bounds, cleared the picket fence, and deposited myself in the corner of the garden to await the result.

The noise, of course, aroused the inmates of the house, and they were soon out with a light, but with no utensils of war except a short double-barreled shotgun, in the hands of my uncle. He inspected the damage done to his favorite bee-stand, and breathed out some rough threats against the villains who had attempt-ed to steal his honey. After ordering his family and the two strangers back into the house, he posted himself in a fence corner about thirty yards off, for the purpose of waging war against the offenders, should they attempt to renew the attack.

The night not being very dark, I was fearful that if I attempted to climb over the picket fence, the old man might pepper me with shot. So I moved myself cau-tiously around to the back part of the garden, and found an opening where a pick-et was missing. Through this aperture I succeeded in squeezing myself, and then crawled around to the rail fence where my uncle was, until I got within two panels of the old man, when I ventured to call him by name, in a very low tone. He knew my voice, and said: "Is that you, Sam?" My answer in the affirmative brought him to where I was, and although the fence was between us, we took a hearty shake of the hand through a crack. He told me that the two men in the house were Union neighbors, who came over to tell him that the trail of a band of bushwhackers had been discovered about six miles from there, and that on to-morrow the whole country would be out in search of them. He told me to go back until his neighbors took their leave, and then to come in and see my mother, who was well, but griev-ing continually about her son "Sam."

I fell back to my companions, reported progress, and again took my stand in the fence corner. As soon as the two neighbors were gone, my uncle made known to my mother, and to his wife and daughters, the cause of the disturbance; the younger members of the family having retired early in the night, were all fast asleep. As soon as my uncle thought it prudent to do so, he came out and invited us in. Although my mother had received the news of my visit with a quiet com-posure, yet, on my approach, she arose silently and started toward me with a firm step, but in a moment she tottered and would have fallen, but I caught her in my arms; she lay with her head on my bosom for some minutes, weeping like a child, and I must confess that now, for the first time since I was a boy, I could not restrain my tears. My mother broke the silence by uttering, in broken sentences: "Oh, my dear son! Have you indeed come to see your mother? I thought I would go down with sorrow to my grave, as I never expected to see you again on earth!" How my manhood and my iron will left me at that moment! How gladly would I have left war and revenge to the beasts of the forest, and secreted myself in some quiet corner of the earth, that there, with my mother and my family, I might once more take delight in the sweet songs of birds, and in the tranquil scenes of life, like those I enjoyed in my younger days!

My mother became more tranquil, and we talked over matters with a great deal of satisfaction; and my uncle, to divert our minds from a subject too serious, occasionally poked fun at me, by accusing me of trying to steal his bee-gum, in which he was joined by my two comrades. His two daughters were flying around in the kitchen, and presently announced a supper for us all. We enjoyed ourselves finely until two o'clock in the night, at which time we were compelled to leave, in order to secure a safe retreat from the vigilant search to be made for us during the following day.

On starting, we rode back on our old trail half a mile, to where we had crossed a small creek, down which we rode, keeping all the time in the water, for about three miles, to a public road leading south, which we followed about six miles; then, on coming to a rocky place where our horses would make no tracks, we left the road at right angles and traveled in the woods about two miles; here we made a semi-circle around a hill, and camped in a commanding position. My comrades did picket duty while I slept nearly all day. At night we went to a friend who lived near my old residence, and from him we learned that our trail had been discovered on our way up, that the whole militia force, composed almost exclusively of my old enemies, together with some Dutch regulars, were quartered at Big River Mills; that the woods were being constantly scoured; that each ford on Big river was guarded night and day, and that they considered my escape impossible.

Before the approach of daylight we secreted our horses in a deep ravine, covered with brush and briars, and then hid ourselves underneath a shelving rock near the top of a high bluff, from which, at a long distance, we had a view of my mother's house—the homestead of the Hildebrand family. We remained here all day, during which time the house was surrounded by soldiers, how many I could not tell, but they seemed to fill the yard and the adjoining inclosures. Presently I saw a dense column of smoke arise from the house, which told me too plainly that the Vandals were burning up the home of my childhood.

The flames presently burst forth through the roof and lapped out their long, fiery tongues at every window. The roof fell in, and all that remained of that superb house was the blackened walls of massive stone.

Gladly would I have thrown myself among those Vandals, and fought them while I had a drop of blood remaining; but it would have been madness, for I would have been killed too soon, and my revenge would have been ended, while my enemies would still live to enjoy their pillage.

Immediately after dark we returned to our horses and commenced our retreat to Arkansas; but instead of going south we traveled west about twenty miles, until we struck on a creek called Forche a' Renault, in Washington county; then turning south, we traveled over the wild pine hills west from Potosi, and camped in a secure place between Caledonia and Webster.

We started on in the evening, and just before sunset made a raid on a store, getting all we wanted, including several bottles of "burst-head." We traveled mostly in the night, followed Black river down to Current river, crossed at Carter's Ferry, and made our way safely to Green county, Arkansas.

CHAPTER X.

Trip with two men.—Killed Stokes for informing on him.—Secreted in a cave on Big river.—Vows of vengeance.—Watched for McGahan.—Tom Haile pleads for Franklin Murphy.—Tongue-lashed and whipped out by a Woman.

After remaining a few days at headquarters I commenced making preparations for another trip against my enemies on Big river. I was yet ignorant of the murder of my brother Henry, and knew nothing about the burning of my mother's house, except what I saw at the distance of a mile, a few hours before I started back to Arkansas. I was now fully determined to use the same weapons upon some of my enemies, and to retaliate by any and all means placed in my power. I told the boys my plan. Among those who were present was Thomas Haile, or "devilish Tom", as he was called, and as usual, he was spinning some of his laughable yarns; but when I spoke the name of Franklin Murphy as probably connected with the house burning, he stopped short in his conversation, and after a moment's reflection he proposed to go with me to see some of his old friends. To this I readily consented, and after selecting another man, we started on our way. We passed through Stoddard and then into Wayne county after a man by name of Stokes. He had fed me on my previous trips, inducing me to believe that he was a substantial Southern man; I learned shortly afterwards that he was laying plans for my capture, and had, more than once, put the Federals on my trail. Notwithstanding I had these statements from good authority, I was unwilling to take his life until I knew to my own certain knowledge that he was guilty. I did not wish to fall into the error, so common among the Federals, of killing an innocent man to gratify the personal enmity of some informer.

Just after dark I went to his house alone, he greeted me in a very cordial manner and remarked:

"Well, Mr. Hildebrand, I'm glad to see you—hope you are well—and are yet too smart for the Feds."

"Are there any Feds in Greenville?"

"None, sir, none at all; I was there to-day; the place is entirely clear of the scamps. By the way, Mr. Hildebrand, are you alone?"

"Oh yes; I am taking this trip by myself."

"Glad to assist you, sir; you must stay with me to-night; I'll hide you to-morrow in a safe place; can go on to-morrow night if you like; would like for you to stay longer."

I thanked him for his proffered assistance, but told him that as I had troubled him so often, I would go to a neighbor's about a mile off and stay until the next night. I went back a short distance to where my men were and waited about an hour.

My two men after putting on the Federal uniform, rode around the place and approached the house from another direction; they rode up in a great hurry and called Mr. Stokes out. Tom Haile in a very confidential tone commenced:

"Well sir! we are on the hot track of Sam Hildebrand! he is here again; he robbed a man down on the Greenville road, five miles below here, about sunset; he came in this direction, and we concluded to ride down to your house thinking that you might have seen or heard something of him."

"I reckon I have, by George! Sam Hildebrand was here not more than an hour ago, and I tried to detain him; he was alone and said he was going to stay until to-morrow night at a certain house; I know the place; hold on a minute! I'll get my gun and coat and will go with you—we've got him this time, sure!"

"All right," said Tom, "come along; we are always glad to meet a man of your stripe."

He marched along with the boys until they came to where I was waiting for them; Stokes had forgotten to ask many questions, but on coming up to me in the dim moonlight he asked, "how many men have you?" one of my men answered "twelve." He at once began laying plans for my capture, and related what he had done on previous occasions "to capture Sam Hildebrand, but that Sam was too sharp for him." When I thought that he had said enough I stopped him with the remark—"I am Sam Hildebrand myself!" and emptied old "Kill-devil" into his bosom.

We then proceeded on, traveling altogether in the night, until about day-break; one morning we got near the ruins of the old Hildebrand homestead, and called at the house of a friend. Knowing that we were in an enemy's country and liable to be trailed, we could not sleep, nor could we travel in the daytime, considering the fact that if our enemies got after us we would have to run about one hundred and fifty miles to get out of their lines, and that the government had no less than four thousand men in active employment all the time for the especial purpose of capturing me. We secreted our horses in a thicket under a bluff and entered a cave near by, which was afterwards called by my name. Our friend remained in the cave a few minutes with us, and it was from him I learned the particulars of the atrocities committed by the Federal troops, in the murder of my poor innocent brother Henry.

I shall not attempt to describe my feelings, when the truth flashed across my mind that all my brothers had been slain in cold blood—Frank, first, and now the other two—leaving me not a brother upon earth except my brother William, who was in the Federal army, but whose well known loyalty was not sufficient to shield his neutral brothers from an indiscriminate butchery. For several hours I remained quietly in the cave, studying the matter over; but finally my mind was made up. I determined to sell my life as dearly as possible, and from that moment wage a war of fire and blood against my persecutors, while one should last, or until I was numbered with the dead.

I hastily gathered my arms; only one word escaped my lips: "Revenge!" sounded and re-echoed from the deepest recesses of the cavern, and with one wild rush I made for the mouth of the cave; but my two men happening to be there, sprang to their feet and choked up the passage; but near it was another outlet—I dashed through it, and down the steep declivity I hastily made my way, and mounted my horse. But Haile was close after me, and before I could pass around a fallen tree he had my horse by the bridle.

"Hold on, Sam! Don't be a fool. If you are going to throw your life away, you cannot expect to kill a dozen; if you take your own time you may kill a thousand! If I go back without you, what could I tell your wife and children? Come, Sam, you must not forget your duty to them. See how they have clung to you! 'Light now, and go with me to the cave."

I have but a faint recollection of going back to our retreat; but when I awoke it was nearly sunset, and Tom soon had me laughing in spite of myself.

When night came we moved our position about five miles, to the residence of William Patton, as he was a man whom I particularly wanted; but we were unsuccessful; he was at home when we first went there, but by some means he succeeded in eluding our grasp. We left there, and before daylight we had secreted our horses in a thicket on Turkey Run, a small creek emptying into Big river above Addison Murphy's, and had stationed ourselves near the residence of Joe McGahan, on the different roads leading to his house. About eight o'clock in the morning I concluded that it was fruitless to watch for him any longer; so I proposed to repair to Franklin Murphy's residence, which was not more than a mile from where we were; but Tom suggested that we must now return to our horses and consult as to our future movements.

We found our horses all right; but when I expressed a desire to stir up Franklin Murphy for being present at the burning of my mother's house, and several other little incidents that led me to think strangely of his conduct, Tom Haile replied:

"I do not believe that he sanctioned, in any manner, the outrages of which you speak; he could not rescue your brother Frank from the hands of a mob who seemed to have the sanction of public opinion; he could not prevent an army of soldiers, acting under the command of another man, from burning the house, nor from killing your brother Henry. Once for all, let me tell you that it will never do for you to attempt to harm that man. He is a member of a certain Order, that dates back for thousands of years; the members are bound together by an obligation to watch over each other's interests, and to shield each other, as much as possible, from any impending danger."

Tom was so sincere, and looked so serious—which was not common with him—that I told him I never would harm one of them, if I knew it, unless it was in self-defense.

We now thought it best to make our way back to Arkansas. We passed through

Farmington and Fredericktown on the following night, and then camped in the woods until evening. We started before night, in order to capture some fresh horses.

Dressed in Federal uniforms, we were riding along the road in Madison county, when on passing a farm, I saw a fine looking horse in a lot near the house. I halted my men, dismounted and went up to the horse to catch him, but he was a little shy, and kept his head as far from me as possible.

While I was thus trying to get a halter on the spirited animal, a woman stepped onto the porch and bawled out:

"See here! What are you trying to do?"

"I'm trying to catch this horse."

"Let him alone, you good-for-nothing! Don't you look pretty, you miserable scamp, trying to steal my only horse?"

"Yes, madam, but I'm afraid you are a rebel."

"I am a rebel, sir, and I'm proud of it! I have two sons in the rebel army, and if I had six more they should all be in it. You white-livered, insignificant scum of creation! you had better let him alone. Why, you are worse than Sam Hildebrand! He wouldn't take the last horse from a poor widow woman!"

By this time I had caught the horse, but as soon as the woman made that last remark, I pulled the halter off, begged her pardon and left.

On getting to headquarters, Tom never let me rest about that adventure.

CHAPTER XI.

Another trip to Missouri.—Fight near Fredericktown.—Horse shot from under him.—Killed four Soldiers.—Went into their camp at Fredericktown and stole four horses.—Flight toward the South.—Robbed "Old Crusty."—Return to Arkansas.

While I was recruiting at our headquarters in Green county, Arkansas, Capt. Bolin and most of his men returned to rest themselves for a while. Of course our time passed off agreeably, for we all had so much to say, and so much to listen to, that the mind was actively engaged all the time, rendering it impossible for time to drag heavily.

Having thoroughly rested myself, on the 25th day of August I selected three men, and we started on a trip to St. Francois county, Missouri. Nothing unusual occurred until we arrived in Madison county. On getting within about eight miles of Fredericktown, daylight overtook us, and we stopped at an old friend's house for breakfast, who had always treated us kindly, for I had stopped with him several times on my previous trips. He stated to us that there were no troops in Fredericktown. Upon receiving this information, from a source, as we supposed, so reliable, we felt quite free, and resolved to make our journey on that day to my old home on Big river. So, after getting our breakfast and feeding our horses, we made our way quietly to our usual place of crossing the gravel road leading from the Pilot Knob to Fredericktown, when we were suddenly fired on from the brush by about fifty soldiers. Fortunately for us, we had not kept the usually travelled path that crossed the road at the place where the soldiers were stationed in ambush; consequently we were about two hundred yards from them, and none of us were hurt, though my horse was shot from under me; the ball that pierced his chest, passing through my pantaloons, slightly burning my knee.

At the word from me my three men whirled into the brush, and we retreated back in the direction from which we came, my men on horses and myself on foot. I was still lame from the effects of the wound received at Flat Woods, but we made good time, and effected our escape. On getting about a mile, I ordered my men to hitch their horses in a thicket, and we would hold the place if they undertook to follow us. After waiting for some time and not hearing from them, we concluded to make our way cautiously back to where we had been fired upon, and try to get a shot. We crept slowly up, and saw six or seven men near the place, but we could not get close enough from the side we were on; so we made our way in the direction of Pilot Knob about a mile, crossed the gravel road behind a hill, and came up on the opposite side.

We got in sight of them just in time to see a party ride up, leading our three horses; at this, I concluded to try one of them at long range, seeing distinctly from our position that we could get no closer without exposing ourselves too much. I pulled off old "Kill-devil" at one of them who wore shoulder-straps; at the crack of the gun the gentleman got a very hard fall, which, I am fearful, killed him. At this they concluded to follow us into our native woods, for which they paid very dearly. They made a dash on us, which caused us to scatter in different directions, to divide their party up into several squads. Each one of us took a course through the woods in the roughest places we could find, which rendered it very difficult for them to follow. I stopped at every place, such as fallen timber, steep banks and high rocks, to get a pop at them, and would be off again in a different direction. Sometimes I was in front, sometimes at one side, and frequently in the rear. I was pleased to see them have so much pluck, for it afforded old "Kill-devil" an opportunity to howl from every knob and dense thicket in the wild woods until about one o'clock in the evening, when they gave up the chase and quit the unequal fight.

On meeting my men, at dark, on the top of a certain high hill designated by me in the morning, I had four new notches on the stock of old "Kill-devil," indicating by that rough record that four more of my enemies had gone to that land where the righteous would cease from troubling them or making them afraid. Two of my men had killed a man apiece, and the other had made what we call in fishing "a water haul." I suppose, however, that he betook himself into some secure corner to meditate on the uncertainty of all human affairs until the danger was over.

The Federals, on the next day, started in search of us with three or four hundred men; but their numbers being so great, we did not make war upon them that day. At night it rained very hard, and whilst it was raining we went into Fredericktown; finding all things quiet about camp, we managed to steal a horse apiece from them, but did not get the saddles and bridles, as we were in a hurry. We got about thirty miles on our way back to Arkansas before morning—each of my men riding bare-backed, with only a halter for a bridle. I stopped, however, at the old gentleman's where we had got breakfast, for the purpose of having a small settlement with him, as he had deceived us in regard to the soldiers at Fredericktown, and, as we believed, had reported us, for we noticed that his son, a lad about fifteen years old, had rode off while we were eating our breakfast on that morning. I stopped, but the old man was not at home, so I took an old saddle and bridle from him, and went on to Arkansas, leaving the Federals to hunt for us, which we were told they kept up about ten days.

Before reaching Arkansas, however, for the purpose of laying in our winter's supplies, we diverged about twenty miles from our usual course to pay our respects to an old Union man living at the crossroads, who had caused the expulsion of two families from the neighborhood by reporting on them.

He still had the remnants of what had once been a full country store. No Federal soldiers happened to be near the premises at the time, so we rode up to his house about sunset, and while I left one man at his door to prevent any one from leaving the house, we went with the old crusty fellow to the store. He was not disposed to be accommodating, but we bought everything that we could put upon our horses and upon a mule that we borrowed of him, and, after telling him to charge it to Uncle Sam, with the Big river mob for security, we left, and before morning were out of the reach of danger. On reaching camp, we relieved the needy, not forgetting the two families that "Old Crusty" had driven from his neighborhood.

CHAPTER XII.

Trip with three men.—Captured a Spy and shot him.—Shot Scaggs.—
At night charged a Federal camp of one hundred men.—Killed
nine men.—Had one man wounded.—Came near shooting James
Craig.—Robbed Bean's store and returned to Arkansas.

My family still remained in Cook settlement, in St. Francois county, Mo., and
as they were in the enemy's country, I did not think it prudent to pay them a visit,
knowing that it would only bring ruin upon them if the fact of my visit should ever
become known to the Unionists in that county. But I determined by some means
or other to effect their escape to Arkansas as soon as it would be prudent to make
the attempt. Capt. Bolin and his men had promised me their co-operation if called
upon for that purpose; but I was well aware that our whole force would be insufficient for the accomplishment of the object, if attempted by force of arms, for two or
three thousand men could be brought against me in less than twenty-four hours.

To keep myself well posted in regard to the strength of the enemy along the
route, I selected three of Quantril's men, and in the latter part of September, started on another raid into Missouri. On arriving at the St. Francis river we found it
swimming, but made no halt on that account, having by this time become inured
to all kinds of hardships and dangers.

On the second day after we started we left the main road and diverged several
miles to our right, for the purpose of traveling in day time. On getting within sight
of a house we discovered some one run into the yard, and immediately afterwards
we saw a little boy running toward a barn. The movement being a little suspicious,
we dashed forward and were soon on each side of the barn. We discovered a man
through a crack, and demanded his surrender; he came to the door and threw up
his hands. On taking him back into the barn, we discovered his bundle to contain
a complete Federal uniform, and when we noticed that the citizen's dress which
he had on was much too small for him, we at once pronounced him a Federal spy.
We found a letter in his pocket, written by a man by the name of Scaggs, to the authorities at Fredericktown, containing the names of his rebel neighbors, whom he
was desirous of having burned out. One of the men in the list I happened to know,
and by that means I knew that Scaggs lived about seven miles from there. We took
the spy half a mile and shot him, then, changing our course, we started on the hunt
for Scaggs, whose residence, however, we did not find until after dark. Dressed
in Federal uniform, we rode up to the gate and called him out. On arresting him
we took him to the house of a friend, who told us that Scaggs had already made
two widows in that neighborhood by reporting their husbands. We took him with

us until daylight appeared, hung him to a limb in the woods, and made our way toward Castor creek, in Madison county.

The next night, on crossing Castor creek, we discovered a camp of Federals; judging them to be about twenty or thirty strong, we concluded to charge them for a few minutes; but on getting into their camp we found that there were three or four times as many as we expected; so we charged on through as quick as possible, still two of our horses were killed and one of my men was slightly wounded in the fleshy part of his thigh. After getting through their camp, we captured the four pickets who were placed in a lane on the opposite side. As we came from the wrong direction, they mistook us for their own men, until we had taken them in. My two men who had lost their horses, now mounted those taken from the pickets. As soon as the pickets told us that they were Leeper's men, we shot them and hurried on.

On our return, at another time, we were told by the citizens that we killed five and wounded several more in our charge through their camp; making nine men killed, including the pickets.

My wounded man could not be kept in Missouri with any degree of safety, and according to the usage of the petty tyrants who commanded the little squads of Federals, it would have been death to any man under whose roof the wounded man might have taken refuge; the man, without any questions asked, would have been shot, his house and property burned, and his wife and children turned out into the world, houseless, forlorn and destitute. To avoid the infliction of such a calamity upon any of our friends, my wounded man was under the necessity of making his way alone back into Arkansas.

My other two men and myself traveled the remainder of the night in the direction of my old home in St. Francois county. I learned that a prolonged effort was made on the following day to trail us up to our camp in the woods; but a rain having fallen about daylight, our tracks were entirely destroyed. On the following night we made our way to the house of a friend, near the ruins of my once happy home. Here I remained, resting myself and scouting over the country on foot, two whole days and nights, trying to shoot some of the miscreants who had belonged to the old mob, but they kept themselves so closely huddled that I had no chance at them.

On the second day, however, while lying near the road, James Craig, captain of the mob—which by this time had assumed the name of Militia—with two men whom I did not recognize, came along, riding very fast. I got a bead on Craig, but my gun did not fire; and I will say here, that this was the only time during the war that old "Kill-devil" deceived me.

On returning to my friend near my old home, he stated to me that our horses, which we had concealed in a nook in one of the bluffs of Big river, had been discovered by some boys who were hunting, and that they had gone to report to the militia. Upon receiving this intelligence, we started at once to our horses, found them all right, and, not being satisfied with the results of our trip, we concluded to obtain some supplies from our good Union friends before leaving. We got on Flat river about the middle of the afternoon, and rode up to a store kept by the sons of John Bean, one of whom belonged to the Vigilance mob—but he was not there.

The boys had sense enough to make no demonstration, so, without damaging anything whatever, I took such things as we needed, in part payment for my property which the mob had destroyed.

The boys looked a little displeased; they considered us bad customers, and did not even take the trouble to book the articles against us.

The militia, having received the report of the boys, mustered their whole force and, on the following day, struck our trail and overtook us between Pilot Knob and Fredericktown; they followed us about ten miles, but only got sight of us occasionally on the tops of hills we had to pass over. Night came, and we neither saw nor heard them any more. We traveled all night and about daylight we rode up to the house of a man named Slater, in the southern part of Wayne county, Missouri, for whom we had been watching for some time. He had made himself very busy ever since the beginning of the war by reporting Southern men. He succeeded in having several of them imprisoned, and their families impoverished. We found him at home; his manhood wilted like a cabbage leaf; we took him about a mile from home and shot him.

We then pursued our way home to Green county, Arkansas, and divided our spoils amongst the destitute families driven there by the ruthless hands of Northern sympathizers.

CHAPTER XIII.

The Militia Mob robs the Hildebrand estate—Trip with ten men.—Attacks a Government train with an escort of twenty men.—Killed two and put the others to flight.

Directly after the termination of my last trip, certain events transpired in St. Francois county of which it is necessary that the reader should be informed. I have already stated that the infamous Vigilance mob finally came to a head by the organization of its worst material into a militia company with James Craig for captain and Joe McGahan for first lieutenant. As Craig could neither read nor write, and did not know his alphabet from a spotted mule, the lieutenant was actually the head and front of the marauders. Their design in assuming the form and style of a militia company was merely for the purpose of legalizing their acts of plunder. They did not pretend to take the field against the Rebels, or to strike a single blow in defense of the State or anything else. While drawing their pay from the government, they spent their time hunting hogs, sheep, and cattle belonging to other people.

Having killed all my brothers but one (and he was in the Union army where they could not reach him), they proceeded to divide the property of the Hildebrand estate among themselves. Mother, though decidedly a Union woman originally, they had long since driven off to Jefferson county, with nothing but her bed and Bible. The homestead had been burned, yet there was an abundance of stock belonging to the estate, and a large field of standing corn.

They collected the stock and gathered the corn, and then proceeded to divide it among themselves. In this division they disagreed very much; a question arose whether an officer was entitled to any more than a private, and a few of them went home declaring that they would not have anything if they could not get their share.

At the very time this valorous militia company had stacked their muskets against the fence and were chasing mother's sheep and pigs around through the dog fennel, I was capturing a government train and getting my supplies in an honorable manner.

About the first of November, 1862, having learned that the Federals were in the habit of hauling their army supplies to Bloomfield from Cape Girardeau on the Mississippi river, Capt. Bolin and myself determined to lay in our supplies from the same source.

We took ten men and started with about ten days' rations. Arriving on a stream called White Water, which, with Castor creek, forms the Eastern fork of St. Francis river, we concealed ourselves in an unfrequented part of the woods. It was necessary that we should be thoroughly posted in regard to the expected time of the arrival of the train, and the probable strength of the escort.

I undertook this delicate mission disguised as a country farmer, in search of a stray mule. Without my gun I made my way on foot to the vicinity of a mill and there concealed myself near a road to await the arrival of some one going to mill. Presently a man came along with a cart and oxen, but I let him pass, fearing that my questions might arouse his suspicions.

I remained there nearly an hour for some boy to pass; at length I saw one at a distance coming slowly along, riding on his sack and whistling little fragments of "John Brown." I stepped into the road before he got near me and walked along until I met him. I asked about my mule, but of course he knew nothing about him. I told him that I had concluded to hunt no further, but that I was anxious to return to Bloomfield if I could only meet with a conveyance for I was tired of walking so much. He told me that the government wagons would pass there on the following day and perhaps I could get a ride. I told him that I would be afraid to do that for the Rebels might capture me; he said that there was no danger of that, for twenty soldiers always went with the wagons.

I returned to my comrades with all the information we wanted, and we soon settled all our preliminary arrangements for the attack. After dark we took the road along which we knew they were to pass; we selected a place called the Round Pond, and secreted ourselves in a clump of heavy timber through which the soldiers could not see, in order that they might imagine the woods full of Rebels.

Night passed and the morning hours wore away, when at length we saw two government wagons coming, and in the sunlight sure enough, twenty bayonets were gleaming.

We suddenly broke from the woods with a great shout, and dashed in among them with all the noise we could make. We fired a few shots, killing two and causing the remainder to break for the woods in every direction. The sole object of our trip being to get supplies of clothing, ammunition, etc., we felt no disposition to hunt them down, but let them continue their flight without any pursuers.

We unhitched the horses and packed them with such things as we needed; after which we burned the wagons and every thing else we could not take with us.

On starting back we went through Mingo Swamp and made our way safely to St. Francis river, which we found out of its banks. With a great deal of difficulty we succeeded in swimming the river with our train, but with the loss of one man named Banks, who unfortunately was drowned. Becoming entangled in a drift of grape vines and brush, he drowned before we could render him any assistance.

CHAPTER XIV.

Federal cruelties.—A defense of "Bushwhacking."—Trip with Capt.
Bolin and nine men.—Fight at West Prairie.—Started with two
men to St. Francois county.—Killed a Federal soldier.—Killed Ad.
Cunningham.—Capt. Walker kills Capt. Barnes, and Hildebrand
kills Capt. Walker.

On arriving at headquarters we busied ourselves for several weeks in building houses to render ourselves as comfortable as possible during the coming winter. Our headquarters were on Crawley's Ridge, between the St. Francis river and
Cash creek, in Green county, Arkansas. It was a place well adapted to our purpose,
affording as it did a safe retreat from a large army encumbered with artillery.

Many of Capt. Bolin's men had their families with them, and our little community soon presented a considerable degree of neatness and comfort. I could
have contented myself longer at this quiet place, but our scouts were constantly
bringing us rumors of fresh barbarities committed by the different Federal bands
who were infesting the country in Southeast Missouri, making it their especial aim
to arrest, burn out, shoot and destroy all those peaceable citizens who from the
beginning had taken no part in the war.

They were especially marked out for destruction who had been known to shelter "Sam Hildebrand, the Bushwhacker," as they were pleased to call me. If any
man should happen to see me passing along the road, and then should fail to
report the same at headquarters, regardless of the distance, he was taken out from
his house and shot, without even the shadow of a trial to ascertain whether he
was guilty or not. An old man, with his head silvered over by the frosts of seventy
winters, who had served his country in many a hard fought battle before his tormentors were born, and who now hoped to go down the declivity of life in peace
and security, found himself suddenly condemned and shot for disloyalty, because
he generously took a stranger into his house for the night, who afterwards proved
to be "the notorious Sam Hildebrand."

These same miscreants, however, would call at any house they pleased, and,
by threats, compel even women, in the absence of their husbands, to cook the last
morsel of food in the house, scraped together by poor feeble women to keep their
children from starving to death.

Did I ever do that? No, never! Did I ever punish a man for feeding a Federal?
Did I ever shoot a man for not reporting to me the fact of having seen a Federal
pass along the road? If that was really my mode of proceeding, I would deserve

the stigma cast upon my name.

My enemies say that I am a "Bushwhacker." Very well, what is a "Bushwhacker?" He is a man who shoots his enemies. What is a regular army but a conglomerate mass of Bushwhackers? But we frequently conceal ourselves in the woods, and take every advantage! So do the regular armies. But a Bushwhacker will slip up and shoot a man in the night! Certainly, and a regular army will slip up and shoot a thousand.

But a Bushwhacker lives by plundering his enemies! So did Sherman in Georgia, and a host of others, with this difference: That I never charged my government with a single ration, while they did so at all times. Besides, I never made war upon women and children, neither did I ever burn a house; while the great marching, house-burning, *no battle hero*, turned his attention to nothing else.

In fact, the "Independent Bushwhacking Department" is an essential aid in warfare, particularly in a war like ours proved to be. There are a class of cowardly sneaks, a gang of petty oppressors — like the Big river mob — who can be reached in no other way. A large regular army might pass through where they were a dozen times without ever finding one of them.

As I stated before, barbarities were committed by a certain band of Federals, that warranted our interference.

Capt. Bolin, myself and nine other men mounted our horses and started on another trip, about the first day of December, 1862.

We crossed the St. Francis, and traveled several nights, until we reached West Prairie, in Scott county, Missouri, where we came upon a squad of Federals, thirty in number, like an old-fashioned earthquake.

Imagining themselves perfectly safe, they had placed out no pickets; so we ran suddenly on them, and before they had time to do any fighting they were so badly demoralized they knew not how to fight.

We killed four, wounded several more, and charged on through their camp, as was our custom; in half an hour we returned to renew the attack, but found nobody to fight.

In our first charge, we caused several of their horses to break loose, which we afterwards got. We had one man wounded, having been shot through the thigh with a Minnie ball. Capt. Bolin and six men took the wounded man back with them to Arkansas, while Henry Resinger, George Lasiter and myself started on a trip to St. Francois county.

One morning, just at daylight, we found ourselves on the gravel road leading from Pilot Knob to Fredericktown, and about seven miles from the latter place. We concealed ourselves in a thicket and watched the road until evening before we saw an enemy. A squad of eight Federals came suddenly in sight, riding very fast. I hailed them, to cause a momentary halt, and we fired. One fell to the ground, but the others hastened on until they were all out of sight. While we were examining our game (the dead man), we discovered three more in the distance, who seemed to have got behind the party, and were riding rapidly to overtake them; at this we divided, taking our stations in two different places for the purpose of taking them in. On coming nearer we discovered that they were not dressed in Federal uniform. We took them prisoners and ascertained that they were Southern sympathizers from near Fredericktown, who had been imprisoned at the Knob for several weeks, but having been released they were on their way home. While we were thus parleying with them, asking questions relative to the forces at the different military posts in the country, the party we had fired into now returned with a much larger force, and suddenly we found ourselves nearly surrounded by a broken and scattered line on three sides of us, at a distance of only one hundred yards. The odds were rather against us, being about sixty men against three. I called quickly to my men to follow me, and we dashed for the uncompleted part of their circle. On seeing this movement they dashed rapidly toward that part and closed the line; but when I started toward that point it was the least of my intentions to get out at that place; I wheeled suddenly around and went out in the rear, contrary to their expectations, followed by my men, shooting as we ran, until we had gained some distance in the woods; having the advantage of the darkness that was now closing in upon us, and being on foot, we escaped from the cavalry, who were tangled up in the brush, and were making the woods resound with their noise.

We luckily escaped unhurt, although there were at least fifty shots fired at us. I received two bullet holes through the rim of my hat, and one through the sleeve of my coat, and one of my men got a notch in his whiskers. We were not certain of having hurt any of the Federals as we passed out of their lines. We kept together and returned to our horses; after a short consultation we mounted and rode back to get a few more shots at them, at long range; but when we got to the battlefield we found no one there. Toward Fredericktown we then made our way, until we got in sight of the place, but saw nothing of the soldiers. During the night we visited several friends, and several who were *not* friends, but did no harm to any one, there being only two men at that time in the vicinity whom we wanted to hang, and they were not at home. On the next day we tore down the telegraph wire on the road to Pilot Knob, and stationed ourselves about a mile from town for the purpose of bushwhacking the Federals when they should come to fix it up; but they were getting cunning, and sent out some Southern sympathizers for that purpose, and we did not hurt them. But I made a contract with one of them for ammunition, and in the evening, when we had again torn the wire down, he came out to fix it up, and brought me a good supply of powder and lead.

From him we learned that a general movement against us was to be made by the troops, both at Fredericktown and the Knob, on the following day.

I knew that the whole country between there and Arkansas was in the hands of the Federals. I knew also that they had learned my trick of invariably making a back movement toward Arkansas, immediately after creating an excitement.

As they seemed not likely to hunt the same country over twice, I concluded to go north of the road and wait a few days until the southern woods were completely scoured, and thus rendered safe for our return.

While waiting for this to be done, I thought it a good opportunity to hunt up a man by the name of Cunningham, who had been living in the vicinity of Bloomfield. During the early part of the war he professed to be a strong Southern man, and had been of some service to our cause as a spy; but during the second year of the rebellion he changed his plans and became to us a very dangerous enemy, and was very zealous in reporting both citizens and soldiers to the Federal authorities.

Our intention on this trip was to arrest and take him to Col. Jeffries' camp, ten miles south of Bloomfield, that he might be dealt with by the Colonel as he might see proper.

On gaining the vicinity of Farmington, where Cunningham now lived, we learned that he was carrying on his oppressive measures with a high hand, and was very abusive to those whom he had in his power.

It is said that he even robbed his own brother, Burril Cunningham, and suffered him to be abused unmercifully by the squad of men under his command. On reaching the Valle Forge we struck his trail and followed on toward Farmington; but some Federals got upon our trail, and would have overtaken us before we reached town, if a friend had not deceived them in regard to the course we had taken.

We found Cunningham at his own house, and when we approached the door I demanded his surrender; he attempted to draw a revolver, and I shot him through the heart.

Having accomplished our object, we now returned to Bloomfield and reported to Col. Jeffries. We remained there about three weeks.

On the 5th day of January, 1863, Capt. Reuben Barnes requested me and my two men to assist him in capturing a man by the name of Capt. Walker, who had a command in the Federal army, and was now supposed to be at his home, about six miles from there.

On approaching the house, Walker ran out, holding his pistols in his hands. As we were near enough, we ordered him to surrender, at which he turned around and faced us. On getting a little nearer, he suddenly shot Capt. Barnes, and started to run. Our chase was soon ended, for I shot him dead.

We took Capt. Barnes back to Bloomfield, where he died the same day. We then returned to Green county, Arkansas, and went into winter quarters.

CHAPTER XV.

Started alone.—Rode off a bluff and killed his horse.—Fell in with twenty-five Rebels under Lieutenant Childs.—Went with them.—Attacked one hundred and fifty Federals at Bollinger's Mill.—Henry Resinger killed.—William Cato.—Went back to Fredericktown.—Killed a man.—Robbed Abright's store.

On the 23d day of January, 1863, I started alone on a trip to Missouri, for the purpose of making some arrangements for the escape of my family to Arkansas. I got along very well until the second night; then as I was riding over a brushy ridge I was suddenly hailed by "Who comes there?"

I halted and in an instant became aware of my close proximity to a Federal camp. I instantly wheeled my horse in the woods to the right; dashed furiously down a steep hill side for a short distance, and then in the darkness plunged over a precipice eight or ten feet high. My horse fell among some rocks and was killed, but I was precipitated a few feet further into a deep hole of water in some creek.

I was a little confused in my ideas for a while, but I had sense enough to crawl up out of the deep water; as I stood there with my dripping clothes I heard some of the soldiers coming down the hill toward me; so I crossed the creek and took up the hill on the other side. I was now completely out of their clutches and could easily have made my escape; but I had left my gun in the deep hole, and the thought of leaving "Kill-devil" in that predicament was more than I could bear.

In a few minutes the soldiers left and went back up the hill. I now slipped back cautiously and got into the water to recover my gun. The water was deep and cold; however, I waded in nearly up to my chin and felt around with my feet for the gun. I got my foot under it finally and raised it up; but I had no sooner got it into my hands than I saw five or six soldiers returning with a light. As they were making their way down through a crevice in the bluff, some ten steps above the rock from which I had been precipitated, I had just time to wade down the creek, which was now only a few inches deep in places, and secrete myself behind a cluster of willows that hung over the edge of the steep bank about twenty yards below.

The Federals remained ten or fifteen minutes, walking around my dead horse, and around the hole of water. They threw the glare of their lantern in every direction, and though I was completely hid from their observation, I must acknowledge that as I stood there in the water, shivering with cold, holding my dripping gun, I felt more like anything else in the world than a major. Finally they struck the trail that I had made up the hill with my dripping clothes and each one of them went in pursuit.

Taking this opportunity I slowly left my retreat and waded down the creek for a long distance. I climbed up the hill on the same side on which the Federals were camped; I made a wide circuit around them and came into the road, some four or five miles ahead. I walked rapidly to keep myself warm, and just before the break of day I arrived at the house of a friend, wet, hungry, and on foot. I was soon supplied with everything I wanted; my gun was well attended to, and when morning came "Kill-devil" looked rather brighter than usual.

I started on in the direction of Fredericktown and fell in with twenty-five Rebel boys, commanded by Lieut. Childs, who asked me to take command of his men and give the Federals a "whack" at Bollinger's Mill, on Castor creek.

That locality for some time had been a place of rendezvous for Southern recruits; that fact being well-known, the Federals concluded to station some men there. They were known to be about one hundred and fifty strong, but I consented on condition that his men all take an oath never to surrender under any circumstances. After the oath was administered we marched to the place above mentioned, arriving there about eleven o'clock at night, on the 4th of February. We succeeded in capturing their pickets, made a charge on their camp, fought them for about five minutes (or until they got ready to fight); killed twenty-two of their number as we were informed afterwards, and at the word we marched out on double-quick time. We took four prisoners with us and got some important information from them, but finding that they were not McNeal's men we released them all.

We lost one man killed, Henry Resinger, and three badly wounded, who recovered.

We carried the wounded with us in our retreat, and at daylight we all started for Mingo Swamp.

The Federals followed us, and as our march was retarded by our wounded; they made their way around and charged us, striking our columns at right angles, they divided our line-cutting off seven of my men, whom they took prisoners.

In this little skirmish I lost one man, and killed three of the Federals, at which they left our trail and permitted us to make our way to St. Francis river, which we were compelled to swim.

We got one horse drowned, but got over safely without any other accident, struck camp and commenced getting our breakfast, dinner and supper, all the same meal. Presently some one from the opposite shore called for us to bring him a horse. From his voice we knew him to be William Cato, one of the seven who had been taken as a prisoner. One of my men swam over to him with a horse, and when he had arrived safely in camp, he informed us that six of the prisoners were shot, and that he had made his escape by dodging them in the brush. He was barefooted, and had torn nearly all his clothing off.

We afterwards learned that the officer in command at Bollinger's Mill was Capt. Leeper from Ironton, Missouri.

Not being satisfied with my trip, I did not remain but one week in camp, before I selected two men and started back to Missouri to make another effort towards getting my family to Arkansas. On getting to Fredericktown we found the place full of soldiers. In that town there lived a Dutchman, whose meddlesome disposition led him to be very zealous in the cause of putting soldiers on the track of private citizens. It seems that he never left town, and that it would be impossible to kill him unless it were done in public.

After night I layed off my coat, and gathering up a saw buck, which I found at a wood pile, I walked straight across a street or two, until I reached the door, thinking thereby not to attract any particular attention; but on being told that he was not at home, I carried myself out of town as soon as circumstances would permit, got with my two men and started on toward Farmington. When morning began to approach we left the road several miles and secreted ourselves on a certain hill, for a friend on whom we had called during the night told us that the military authorities were aware of my presence in the neighborhood, and that they had secured the services of two or three good woodsmen to aid in tracking me up.

About one o'clock in the afternoon we discovered a man tracking us slowly around our steep hill, looking cautiously ahead, holding his gun in a position to raise and fire in an instant. The ground was hard and our horses were not easily trailed, but our pursuer kept moving along very slowly. We were at a loss to know whether he was really a brave man or a natural fool. Not coming to any definite conclusion however, I concluded to make my way down the hill a little to gratify his curiosity by letting him find me. I wounded him severely on purpose to let him see me, but he yelled so loud that I had to kill him with my knife, for I wanted "peace" about that time.

We heard some horsemen coming, so we hastened away from there and secreted ourselves in a thicket on Wolf creek, near the residence of John Griffin.

Here I learned that my wife had procured a little wagon and a small yoke of oxen, with which to move to Arkansas; that she started with the family on the 16th day of February, and by this time was in the vicinity of Bloomfield.

At night we went out on the plank road leading from Farmington to Ste. Genevieve and fired into a camp of Federals; we could not get near enough to do them any harm, but wished to draw them out to hunt for us; but in this we failed and had to abandon the project.

From there we went to the junction of the Pilot Knob and Iron Mountain roads, and robbed a store belonging to a Dutchman by the name of Abright We patronized him very liberally and started back to Arkansas with all the goods we could pack.

At this stage of the war the Federals held possession of all the principal places in Southeast Missouri. Bloomfield was also held by them, and there was no doubt in my mind but what my family was now in their hands.

While passing through Stoddard county, the Federals overtook us, and run us so closely that we were compelled to throw off a part of our loads; on arriving at

St. Francis river we found it guarded. Our only chance was to whip the Federals, and we determined to try it. We retreated into a dense cane brake and then commenced upon them. We killed three of their men on the second round and then they fled. We got home safely and were again prepared "to clothe the naked and feed the hungry."

CHAPTER XVI.

Started to Bloomfield with three men.—Fight at St. Francis River.—
Starts on alone.—Meets his wife and family.—They had been ordered off from Bloomfield.—Capture and release of Mrs. Hildebrand.—Fight in Stoddard county.—Arrival in Arkansas.

For the purpose of getting my family to Arkansas, it was necessary that I should make a trip to Bloomfield, although that place was now held by a large Federal force under McNeal.

I started with three good men, crossed the St. Francis river at a shoal, but we had not proceeded more than ten miles when we ran into a company of McNeal's men, who instantly fired upon us, slightly wounding one of my men in the fleshy part of his arm.

We thought it best for four men to retreat from the fire of nearly one hundred, which we did, in double-quick time. They pursued us very closely, but were at too great a distance for them to shoot us.

Wishing to get a few shots at them, we concluded to cross the river and give them a fight from the other side; so we plunged our horses in the deep water at the nearest point, were swimming, and had nearly gained the opposite shore, when the Federals ran onto the bank we had just left and fired a volley at us with their muskets; but their shots were all too high.

We reached the bank where the willows were very thick, jumped off our hors-es and returned the fire. From our place of concealment we could easily see that three of their number were killed. They kept up a random fire at the willow thick-et, in which they wounded three of our horses and caused them to run up into the woods, terribly affrighted. By this time they had ceased firing and had taken refuge behind trees, and were watching for our movements; in this position they stood two rounds from our rifles, in which four of them fell, having been shot through the head. Before we could get another shot we discovered a portion of the men making their way up the river, and I understood at once that their intention was to engage our attention at that place, while a part of the command would make their way around and take us in; so we retreated in good order to a place of safety, and remained all night.

The next morning we crossed the river in company with several others and found that the Federals during the night after the fight had gone to Bloomfield. They procured a wagon and team from an old man living near for the purpose of hauling off their dead. The old man stated to us that there were seven killed and two wounded.

I now decided to change my tactics, and try my luck alone and on foot. I thought that by stealthy movements I could find my family and get them off to Arkansas much better than with a small company of men.

In a few days I met my family about twenty miles south from Bloomfield on their way to Arkansas, in an old wagon pulled by a small yoke of oxen, which my wife was driving. I learned from her that some of Capt. Bolin's men had removed her from Flat Woods to Bloomfield, in Stoddard county, Missouri, but that Mc-Neal, on taking possession of the town, had ordered her to leave, adding that the wife and family of that "desperado, Sam Hildebrand," could not remain within one hundred miles of his headquarters.

With the wagon and oxen furnished her by a friend to our cause, she took the children and some provisions and started out upon the road, and when I met them she was making her way as best she could, but was just preparing to camp for the night in the lone woods. She cautioned me very particularly about the Federals, and said that she had seen two or three squads that day. On the following morning we resumed our journey, and about ten o'clock I met six Union soldiers, who came suddenly upon me at a short turn in the road, but, being dressed in Federal uniform, they did not suspicion me as being a Rebel. They asked me to what command I belonged, and I answered them to Capt. Rice's, stationed at that time in Fredericktown; at this they seemed satisfied, and passed on, swearing vengeance against any Rebels that might fall in their way.

As soon as they were out of sight, I told my wife to drive on, while I traveled through the brush awhile. I had scarcely got out of the road when I discovered a whole regiment of Federal soldiers, not more than half a mile off, who were coming directly toward us. I soon gained an eminence in the woods, from which I could observe their maneuvers. They stopped at the wagon, and after parleying with my wife for several minutes, they turned her team around and took my family along.

At this juncture it is needless to say that I became enraged, and knowing an old rebel citizen about two miles off, I resolved at once to go to him, thinking that perhaps I might hear from some of our boys, for I was sure that if there were any in the neighborhood the old man would know it. I was overjoyed when he told me that James Cato and Wash Nabors were taking a nap in the barn, while he was standing on the lookout. I repaired to the barn at once, told them the fate of my family, and that I wanted their assistance that we might amuse ourselves in bush-whacking them.

After getting something to eat, and some provisions to take along with us, we started through the dense forest, and got in sight of them about sundown. Before darkness set in we killed a man apiece, and then lurked around the camp all night. About every two hours, Cato, Nabors and myself would meet at a certain hill, designated before dark, and report progress. I made a great many random shots, but I think that during the night I killed as many as fifteen men. My comrades thought that they both together killed as many more. I learned afterwards that the number we killed during the night was just thirty; none were wounded that I ever could hear of.

Morning began to approach, and we fell back to a high hill, until they began to move toward Bloomfield. Throughout the day they kept their skirmish lines so strong that we could do nothing; however, we got several shots, at long range, at their scouts, but during the entire day I was not certain of killing more than two men.

We kept in the woods, as near the troops as we could, until we had followed them into the very suburbs of Bloomfield; then we started back along the road about dark, intending to pick up stragglers. Judge of my surprise and joy when, on going back, I came across my wife and children sitting by the roadside, where the Federals had left them about noon, but without the oxen and wagon, and without any provisions, bedding or change of clothing.

The capture of my wife had proved rather fatal to them, and her detention among them had produced nothing but disaster and death.

It reminded me of a passage of Scripture that I once heard my mother read from the Book of Samuel, giving an account of the Philistines having captured the ark of the covenant; they took it from one place to another, but a plague was produced wherever it was detained, until many thousands were dead. Finally, to get it out of their hands, they hitched up a yoke of cattle to a cart, and without any driver started it out of the country. The Federals, however, varied somewhat from the Philistines, for, instead of giving her a cart and oxen, and loading her down with presents of gold, they took her wagon and oxen and everything else she had, and left her by the roadside in an unknown wilderness.

On seeing me my family was greatly relieved in mind, yet they were in a starving condition, and we had nothing to divide with them. Believing that the "ark" might have been left there for the purpose of trapping me, I took my position about two hundred yards from my family, and remained while my two comrades were gone after something for them to eat. After their return I made a fire for my wife in the woods, and gave her directions in regard to the course she must travel in the morning, in order to reach the house of our old friend. After bidding them adieu, I was forced to leave them in their forlorn condition. We hastened on to our old friend and requested him to meet my family as early as possible, and convey them to his house. He did so; and in the evening of the same day, having procured the use of a team, we started on for Arkansas.

Col. McNeal sent out a party from Bloomfield, under Capt. Hicks, who followed us to the St. Francis river, but we had got across, and they did not venture very close to the bank, having learned a lesson from me on my upward trip a short time before.

We arrived safely at Capt. Bolin's camp, and my family was soon safely housed and supplied with the necessaries of life, in the charming little community where a score of pleasant families resided.

CHAPTER XVII.

Put in a crop.—Took another trip to Missouri with six men.—Surrounded in a tobacco barn.—Killed two men in escaping.—Killed Wammack for informing on him.—Captures some Federals.—and releases them on conditions.—Went to Big River Mills.—Robbed Highley's and Bean's stores.

Having succeeded in getting my family to Green county, Arkansas, I settled on a piece of land whose owner had left for parts unknown, intending to hold the same until the owner should return. During the month of April, 1863, I was an "honest farmer," and by the 10th day of May I finished planting a field of corn, while at the same time my wife put in a large garden.

At this occupation I enjoyed myself very well for a while; I got some chickens, a few pigs, and a milch cow, so that my family could get along without materially interfering with my main object in life—that of killing my enemies.

The boys were now anxious to make another trip to Missouri; so I took six men and started for Castor creek, in Madison county, after some notorious scamps who had been giving us trouble on previous trips, by putting the Federals on our trail, besides the constant annoyance they gave Southern citizens in that country, by reporting them to the Federals.

We passed west of Bloomfield through the Southern part of Madison county, arriving in the neighborhood about daylight on the morning of the fourth day from home, secreted our horses, leaving three men to guard them, while myself and the others proceeded to spy out the men for whom we had come in search. We did not succeed in finding any of them, and after returning to our camp in the woods at sunset, we went to an old friend's about three miles distant, where we could get a night's sleep, and something to eat for ourselves and horses.

On arriving, our old friend received us kindly, but told us that as he was not well we would be under the necessity of taking care of our own horses, which we were very willing to do. After supper we tied our horses in a neighboring thicket; but as the weather was rather inclement, we repaired to an old tobacco barn for shelter; it was about one hundred yards from the woods on one side, and about two hundred on the other. Here we slept soundly, keeping one man on watch all the time, but as we had not slept more than one hour in each twenty-four since starting, our sentinel fell asleep. In the morning I went out to take a peep at the weather, and was saluted by a shot that struck a board just above my head. I sprang into the barn, raised the alarm, and took a peep at the position of our enemies. They were about thirty strong, and had completely surrounded the barn, posting themselves behind stumps and old trees, but at a distance of about one hundred and fifty yards.

The extent of their circle made their lines very weak, and perceiving that they were much the strongest in front of the barn, I ordered my men to remove the underpinning from one place in the rear of the house. We crept through this aperture, and lay on the ground at the back of the building, being protected from observation by a pile of rubbish. I proposed taking the lead, and directed my men to follow in a straight line, but to keep twenty or thirty feet apart. I arose and started at full speed; but before I got fifty yards, all the Federals who were in sight of me, fired off their guns; yet I was not killed, but felt a stinging sensation on the point of my shoulder, which afterwards proved to be a slight abrasion, caused by a musket ball. On reaching the line, I shot the two men with my revolver who were guarding that point, without making the least halt; but I could not help feeling a thrill of pity for them and wished that they were again alive and on my side, for they were brave men and faced the music nobly, but missed their aim.

My men followed me through to the woods unhurt, save one poor fellow, who was pierced by a musket ball just as he reached the edge of the timber.

On reaching the woods, which were very thick, we felt much relieved, and were quite at home. We reached our horses, and fearing that the Federals might find them, we mounted and rode back to give them a little brush; but finding them all gone, we made our way around to our friend in whose barn we had slept, but found that the Federals had killed him, and had committed many other depredations about the place before leaving. Our kind lady, who had thus so unexpectedly been made a widow, was suffering the pangs of uncontrollable sorrow, but from her broken sentences we learned that a citizen by the name of Wammack was with the soldiers, and was probably the informant at whose instigation the whole tragedy had been brought about, and that as the soldiers left in the direction of Fredericktown, he took the road toward his house. We concluded to try, and if possible, to get Wammack. I ordered three of my men to take the horses out of the neighborhood, to travel over ground where they would occasionally make plain tracks, until they got to a certain creek, eight or ten miles off, then to turn back, keeping in the creek some distance, and then to secrete themselves in the bushes near the residence of one Mr. Honn. Our arrangements having been completed, we separated; myself and my two men had not proceeded far, keeping all the time near the road, before we discovered three men coming from the direction of Wammack's house. When they were near us, we hailed them, and leaving our guns, we stepped out into the road where they were and inquired the way to Cape Girardeau. We told them that we had obtained furloughs at Ironton the day before, and were on our way to Illinois to see our families, but that a few miles back we met some soldiers, who stated that they had got into a skirmish with the bushwhackers and were going to Fredericktown to bring out the whole force; so we concluded to hide in the woods until they returned.

They mistook us for Federal soldiers, sure enough, and one of them related the whole circumstance in a very jubilant manner, stating that he was with the soldiers at the time, that they had killed four of the bushwhackers and the old Rebel who had harbored them, and that if he had his way he would burn up the whole premises. I suggested that we had better go to the main road and wait until the force came; but he objected, for the reason that he wished to see who buried the dead bushwhackers.

By this time I thought I could venture to ask him his name, and after telling me that his name was Wammack, and that he was "all right," he made a motion to proceed, at which we drew our revolvers and told him that he was a prisoner. The other two having answered a sign which I made while talking to Wammack, I saw that *they* were "all right" instead of him. I told them that they could go, but requested them to bury the dead, which they cheerfully agreed to do.

Just as this conversation ended, Wammack suddenly jerked out his revolver and attempted to shoot one of my men and broke to run; the movement was so sudden and so unexpected that he got nearly forty yards before we succeeded in killing him.

We then left that part of the country and went to Wayne county; while stopping there for supper at the house of an old Rebel, a young man came in and stated that about five miles from there, on Lost creek, he saw some Federals putting up for the night; on receiving this pleasing information, we determined to go and take them "out of the wet," as one of my boys expressed it, and after feeding our horses and taking our rations, we were soon on our way for that purpose.

We found the place without much difficulty, made our way to the house and knocked at the door. The man of the house came, and in answer to our questions, stated that there were five Federals sleeping in the stable loft, and that their horses were in the stable. After telling the old man who we were, and ordering him not to leave the house, we proceeded to surround the stable, which stood in the middle of a lot of perhaps about half an acre. Our positions having been taken, I set fire to a hay stack that stood in the corner of the lot, nearly in front of the stable door. When the hay blazed up, the light shone so suddenly on the Federals that they sprang to their arms in a great fright. I hailed them, demanding their surrender, and told them that I was Sam Hildebrand, and that I and my twenty men had them completely in our clutches, but that if they would surrender without firing a gun, I would let them off on easy terms. To this they gladly acceded, and coming down from the loft, they piled their arms in the lot. I ordered two of my men to extinguish the fire that had caught in the fence, and then proceeded to negotiate with our prisoners, which was done in a friendly and satisfactory manner. Rough jokes were passed back and forth with perfect freedom, and they repeated some of the many tales of blood circulated in camps about me, in which I was represented as a hero more daring and dreadful than "Jack the Giant Killer."

At this time there were two of Capt. Bolin's men in prison at Ironton, who had been captured while on a scout up Black river in Reynolds county, Missouri; and as my prisoners belonged to the command stationed at that place, I proposed to them that if they would pledge themselves that by some means or other they would manage to let the two boys escape, we would release them, and permit each one to retain his private property. To this they agreed; they retained their pistols, but gave up their guns and horses.

We all stayed until morning, took breakfast together with the old man, who seemed highly pleased at the turn matters had taken, and occasionally contributed to our fun by some of his timely jokes.

After breakfast we separated, the Federals making their way on foot, carrying a pass from me, written by one of my men, to prevent any of our boys from molesting them on their way, should they happen to fall into their hands.

After a short consultation with my men, we concluded that it was about time to make our enemies in St. Francois county pay their taxes to the Southern Confederacy. On the evening of the last day of May, we rode into the little town at Big River Mills, and made a haul on the store of John B. Highley, but not being certain of his politics, we were very light on him. We then went six miles further to John Bean's store on Flat river, arriving there about 11 o'clock in the night. We knew him to be a strong Union man, and we knew also that one of his sons belonged to the Big river mob. We supplied ourselves with such articles as were needed by the families at Capt. Bolin's camp.

In a few days after our arrival in Green county, the two boys who had been in prison at Ironton, came in, and related to us that the guards who permitted them to escape, told them all about the contract they had entered into with me. Those Federals deserve much credit for keeping their word.

CHAPTER XVIII.

Took seven men.—Went to Negro Wool Swamp.—Attacked fifteen
or twenty Federals.—A running fight.—Killed three.—Killed
Crane.—Betrayed by a Dutchman.—Hemmed in a house by Federals.—Fight and escape.—Killed eight soldiers.—Caught and
hung the Dutchman.

Concluding to take a trip to Negro-Wool Swamp, I selected seven good men,
and struck out; making our way slowly, we visited our Southern friends, and
passed off the time very pleasantly with them. We made but few miles a day until
nearing the point to which we had started, the object of our trip being to take in
a couple of very noisy Union men, for the purpose of giving them a nice necktie
of our own make, manufactured from the textile fabric of nature's own production that we occasionally stripped from the thrifty young hickories in the shady
woods. But while we were on the lookout for them, a scout of Yankees, fifteen or
twenty in number, came into the neighborhood, and we concluded to let the two
meddlesome Unionists rest for the present and to give the Federals a chase. We
ascertained their exact locality, and at sundown I gave one of them a dead shot
from old "Kill-devil," which was all that was necessary to give them a start, and I
assure you it was "a running start."

Seeing the course they took, we knew that they were bound for Bloomfield, so
we mounted and started in pursuit; but they knew so well who was after them that
they gave us no show for a fight; however, being much better acquainted with the
country than they were, I made my way, with one of my men, across on a nearer
route, and got in ahead of them, while my other boys kept up the chase. We did
not beat them much, for when we had gained the point, we heard them coming at
full speed, and as they passed, we both fired at the same time; only one man fell,
and as "old Kill-devil" was in the habit of tearing a tolerable large hole, we had
no dispute about who did it. From there on to within a few miles of Bloomfield,
our chase was in vain; a streak of greased lightning could hardly have caught
them. Knowing that a considerable force would now be sent out into the vicinity
of Negro-Wool Swamp to clear that country of bushwhackers, we concluded not
to return to that place, but wound our way around south of Bloomfield, and ran
suddenly on to a man by the name of Crane, for whom one of Capt. Bolin's men
had been hunting for more than a year; as he was not along, and we were acting as
a band of brothers, I took it upon myself to shoot the *fowl*. After having done so, we
made our way into Wayne county, where we remained several days, enjoying the
rich luxuries placed at our disposal by our friends in that country. We then took

a scout on Black river, and stopped with a German, who had always professed great friendship for us, and who, on this occasion, greeted us very warmly, and seemed to put himself to a great deal of inconvenience to make us comfortable; he stood watch for us, as usual, while we slept in an unoccupied house. Our minds being free from suspicion, we slept quite soundly for three or four hours, but I was aroused by the sound of horses' feet; and by the time I had awakened my men, and made ready for our escape, we were completely surrounded. Through a crack I took a hasty peep, and saw our old friend, the German, on horseback and in the line of the Federal soldiers.

At this juncture, two of my men were in favor of surrendering; I answered by telling them to follow me. There being a dense forest in front of the house, not more than one hundred and fifty yards off, I made for it in my fleetest manner, holding my gun in my left hand and my revolver in my right; I would have killed the Dutchman as I ran, but he was on the opposite side of the house; a whole volley was fired at us as we went, killing one of my men and wounding two more slightly, but not sufficiently to disable them from duty, and giving me four very slight wounds. As we passed out, we fired two or three shots a piece with our revolvers, killing two of their horses, and wounded one man seriously in the face.

On gaining the woods we felt very well over our narrow escape, and made our way for a gap in the bluff, about half a mile off, through which we knew the Federals could not easily ride; we gained the point, stopped to rest ourselves, and reloaded our pistols; after which we made our way to the top of the bluff, and discovered through the thick brush, at a distance of not more than two hundred yards, the Federals approaching slowly and cautiously toward us. I gave my men orders to fire in the same order in which they lay, that is for our extremes to fire on theirs, so that no two men would fire at the same Federal.

When fairly within gun shot I gave the word and we fired; four of them fell dead, and one fellow, badly wounded, broke down the hill calling loudly on the name of the Lord. Our rifles were quickly reloaded and we followed cautiously after them in the direction of our friend's house where we came so near being taken in; on gaining the edge of the woods we discovered them sitting on their horses, near the house from which we had escaped. They seemed to be holding a council of war; one of them who had on shoulder-straps, appeared to be making a speech. The distance being about one hundred and fifty yards some of my men objected to shooting, but I answered by giving the word slowly, "ready,—aim,—fire!" At the discharge of our rifles, four of them fell, and the gentleman with shoulder-straps was helped from his horse. At this juncture, they began to form themselves into about twenty different lines, with only one abreast, each man being in advance, and each one bringing up his own rear. It was a novel military position, a kind of "nix cum rous," but it worked well and in almost an instant they seemed to be spirited away, and we saw no more of them.

STAMPEDE OF FEDERAL SOLDIERS

We made our way down Black river about two miles and camped for the night, and the next morning about sunrise I went to the house of a friend, who lived back in the woods to obtain provisions for my men. He told me that the Federals had left for Greenville immediately after our second round at them, and had given orders to some citizens to bury their dead, and on the following day to send the horses to Patterson, which they left in their care, and which included those they had captured from us; at which place they would meet them with a large force and proceed to exterminate the Bushwhackers.

I obtained what provisions we wanted and hastened back to camp. After eating we hurried over to the Patterson road, selected a good position, and waited impatiently for the men to come along with the horses. About ten o'clock in the forenoon an old man about sixty years of age, and three little boys came slowly along with them. After they had approached sufficiently near, we stepped out and I addressed the old man in a very friendly manner, and stated our business, at which he made some serious objections, remarking as he removed his old cobpipe, that it was rather against his orders, "to deliver the horses up to Sam Hildebrand." As the old man gave the horses up, I could easily perceive a smile of secret satisfaction lurking about his face. The little boys, however, were badly scared, and seemed to realize the fact that Sam Hildebrand had them. We took possession of the horses, fourteen in number, and according to previous arrangements, five of the boys struck for Green county, Arkansas, with them, while one of them stayed with me, on foot, for the purpose of killing the German who had betrayed us, and thus came so near having us taken in, and who had caused one of the bravest men in the Southern Confederacy, to be killed. After sending the old man and the boys away I took leave of my men, and with my comrade repaired to a neighboring hill, rested and slept by turns, until near sunset.

From the position we occupied I had a fair view of the surrounding country, and particularly the main road leading to Patterson. But during the day all was quiet, save when a citizen would occasionally pass along the road.

As night approached we became restless from inaction, and before the sun had shed its last rays upon the neighboring hills we were on our way to the scene of our tragedy the day before.

Arriving there before it was entirely dark we took our position in the fence corner near the house, and here we lay in silent impatience until the gray horizon warned us that our watch for the present was ended. We quietly retired to the house of a friend for our breakfast, not having eaten anything except a piece of corn bread since the morning before. Having partaken heartily of our friend's rough but substantial fare, we again repaired to the house of our treacherous German enemy, having sworn in our wrath to take his life before leaving the country, and succeeded in gaining a position within one hundred yards of his house and directly in front of the door. Here we remained all day, during which time the family seemed to be discharging their domestic duties very cheerfully. About four o'clock in the afternoon two strange men rode up to the house and held a conversation with the lady for several minutes and then rode off in the direction they came, this gave us some hope that the Dutchman would soon be at home. It was evident that as he had left with the Federals the day before in their retreat, and in great haste, that he had made no arrangements for a long absence; and it was more than probable that those two men only came to see whether or not the way was clear. We felt indeed that our most sanguine expectations were soon to be realized; but the hour passed slowly on; we changed our position after dark to a place in the fence corner, near the woodpile, and here we remained until the night was half spent. Then we were made glad by the sound of horses' feet coming from the direction of Patterson; as the sound came nearer we could easily perceive that the noise was made by only one horse.

Advancing slowly, the Dutchman approached the house, alighted at the woodpile and tied his horse to the end of one of the limbs within a few feet of us. Just then we arose and demanded his surrender. The old fellow was very badly alarmed and called alternately on the Almighty and Mr. Hildebrand for mercy; but I gave him to understand that it was useless for him to beg for mercy; that he was a prisoner and that we expected to take him to headquarters as a prisoner of war. His wife came out to the fence immediately on his arrival, and it was her presence alone that prevented us from shooting him on the ground.

I guarded him while my comrade went to the stable to look for another horse; but finding nothing there but an old mule, he came back leading it with a blind bridle.

I requested the lady to loan me a saddle, and she soon returned with her own side saddle, and remarked that it was the only saddle on the place. I told her I could not rob a lady; to keep the saddle, and that I was sorry from my heart to be compelled to give her uneasiness or trouble; that war had no mercy, and that through it all I hoped that she would be protected from harm.

We tied the old man's hands behind him, and then tied him on the mule without any saddle; at which the mule humped up his back, gave us a specimen of mule melody on a base note that re-echoed among the hills, and then became more quiet. We started on leading the horse and mule, but we had to stop several times to let the mule finish braying, for he would not budge an inch until he got entirely through. We went about a mile and then proceeded to hang the Dutchman. He spoke only once and then the mule chimed in, and before he had finished, the Dutchman was swinging to a limb. To render his duplicity still more apparent, it should be borne in mind that he was now completely dressed in Federal uniform, having probably enlisted during his absence. Previous to the hanging, we had taken from him his pocket book and a revolver.

We now mounted the horse and mule, and went on about two miles, stopped at the house of a friend and called for something to eat. Our friend, on hearing what had taken place, plead manfully for the lady whom we had so lately made a widow, stating that she was a good woman, recounted many good deeds she had performed, and finished by adding that she would now be entirely dependent on the charity of the community for support, and insisted on us having the horse and mule sent back.

We readily consented to this, and told him also that we would much rather she had the pocket book also, for on counting the money we found that it contained forty dollars.

No one could deliver the mule, horse and money to her without being considered in some measure implicated. Finally it was agreed for our friend to take the horse and mule back while it was yet night; to leave them near the premises and to throw the pocket book over the gate into the yard. All things being arranged we started on foot for our homes in Arkansas, and arrived there safely.

CHAPTER XIX.

Took eight men.—Attacked a Federal camp near Bollinger's Mill at
night.—Lost two men killed and one wounded.—His men return
to Arkansas.—He went alone to St. Francis county.—Watched the
farm of R. M. Cole to kill him.—Was checked by conscience.

I remained two weeks at home plowing, and then went on a scout to the vicinity of Mingo Swamp with eight men. We watched around for several days to capture some infamous scamps in that country who had been giving our friends trouble from the beginning of the war. Being too cowardly to go into the army, they were staying at home and were constantly annoying peaceable citizens by making false reports against them of every kind.

Having failed to get any of them, we concluded to make another trip over onto Castor Creek, for my men were always anxious to go to parts of the country frequented by the Federals. We had been on Castor but one day and night when a party of Federals came along, making their way through the country, and camping within a short distance of Bollinger's Mill. We were quietly enjoying ourselves in the nook of rocky range of brushy hills when a runner came to inform us of the fact. Of the exact number of the Federals he did not know.

It was with some difficulty that I restrained my men to wait until a proper hour of the night before making the attack, but finally about ten o'clock I gave the word to get ready, which was done in a very few minutes. Going around the hills we struck the main road about a mile from their camp. We rode very slowly until we routed the pickets, then dashed on and crowded them into camp; but the locality of their camp and the position in which they had taken up quarters, had not been stated to us correctly; consequently we came out somewhat worsted.

They had chosen a narrow place in the road, and had turned their wagons across it, so that in our attempt to dash through their camp, as was our custom, we found our progress suddenly stopped; this bothered us so badly that they opened a heavy fire on us, killing two of my men and wounding another slightly before we had time to retreat. We were not certain of having killed any of them, but were afterwards told by a citizen that we wounded three, one of whom died next morning. After this unfortunate mistake my remaining men wanted to go back to Green county, Arkansas, where our wounded companions could be properly cared for; to which I consented, and bidding them adieu I started alone to St. Francois county, Missouri.

I now thought this a favorable opportunity to take vengeance upon R. M. Cole for the course he had taken at the time my brother Frank was hung by the Big river mob. That matter had never yet been redressed, and my mind was yet harrassed by conflicting impressions concerning his guilt or innocence in the matter. That he was a Southern man I very well knew, but that it was his duty, as a civil officer, to wrest my brother from the clutches of a merciless mob I knew equally well. I will here remark that all my evil impressions concerning his complicity in the hanging of my brother have long since been entirely removed from my mind; but at time of which I am now writing, I finally adopted the unwelcome conclusion that he was evidently guilty. I escaped the vigilance of my enemies, and of the hundreds of soldiers whose especial duty it was to watch out for me; and unobserved by any one who would be likely to inform against me, I succeeded in reaching his farm, on Flat river, and found to my joy that he had not yet finished plowing. I went around to the back part of the farm, hitched old Charley to a sapling in the woods, and taking old "Kill-devil" in my hand, I cautiously approached the cornfield where I had seen him plowing from a distance, and about sunset I secreted myself in a fence corner about ten rows from where he had plowed the last furrow. I waited until I became satisfied that he had stopped for the night. It was now about dark.

I went back to where I had hitched my horse, unsaddled him and went in search of feed. I soon found an abundance of oats already cut in the field. On my way back I chanced to cross a splendid melon patch; on the ripe melons I made out my supper, feeling thankful for my good luck so far.

My only chance now was to wait until morning, which I did, making myself as comfortable as possible during the night.

In the morning I took my station again in the fence corner with old "Kill-devil" already cocked. After a long delay, as I thought it, he made his appearance, following along behind the plow and singing most merrily. I was a little flustrated by his merry mood, and a strange weakness kept me from firing. I thought I would let him plow one more round. How I chuckled to myself as he walked deliberately away from me as if nothing was about to go wrong with him. He came around again as merrily as before. I once more raised old "Kill-devil" to my face and was in the act of pulling the trigger, when I heard a stick crack in the woods just as he was turning. This and some other imaginary noises caused me to delay until he was too far off to make a sure shot. Here was a good chance lost. This I thought would never do, for I was now becoming quite nervous; I bit my fingers as I usually do to stop what hunters call the "buck ague," but it seemed to do me no good.

The more I thought of the matter, the more nervous I got, and I must acknowledge that I never felt that way before when I was in a just cause, and a thought struck me that there might be something wrong in this matter after all. I knew that it would never do to remain squatting in the fence corner any longer; that I must either shoot or leave.

Can it be possible that he is innocent of the charge brought against him by my friends, and that my suspicions are groundless?

It may be so! I began to think about letting the man live; but the thought of riding several hundred miles for the express purpose of killing a man, and then to go back without doing it, after having had such a good chance, was a thought that I did not like.

While these thoughts were revolving in my mind I still set as quietly as a mouse. Once I would have got up and left, but the man was now making his third round, and was too close for me to do so without being seen. I deliberately raised my gun and took a bead on him to make my decision while he was completely in my power—"live on, sir! live on!" was my decision, and as soon as he turned I hastily left for fear of being tempted again. I mounted my horse, and as soon as I thought he was out of sight among the corn I rode away, and never before in my life did I feel so happy as I did when I passed opposite the row he was in. I bade him a silent farewell, and mentally told him to rest easy, for that he never should be hurt by my hand.

On my homeward trip I stopped in the vicinity of Bloomfield (which was still in the hands of the Federals) in order to pay my respects to Captain Hicks. He was the commander of the company which followed me and my family to the St. Francis river; and boasted that he was the man who shot me at the Flat Woods. Not being disposed to rob him of his honors, I was willing to admit that he did the act, and to govern myself accordingly.

I lay around his residence four days and nights, getting my provisions out of his smoke-house, before he made his appearance.

On the evening of the fourth day he rode up to his house, and in a few minutes walked out with his wife into the garden.

I walked up to the garden fence and spoke to him; he seemed agitated and started toward the house; I raised my gun, halted him, and told him to come to me as I wanted to talk a little to him. He halted and with some reluctance walked toward me, and on getting within a few paces he asked me who I was. I told him that I was Sam Hildebrand; that I understood he had been hunting for me for some time, and I thought I would come by and see what he wanted. At this he made a lick at me with a hoe which he held in his hand, and came very near hitting me; but in a moment I ended his existence by shooting him. I eluded all search and effected my escape to Arkansas.

CHAPTER XX.

Trip to Hamburg with fifteen men.—Hung a Dutchman and shot another.—Attacked some Federals in Hamburg, but got gloriously whipped.—Retreated to Coon Island.—Return to St. Francis river.—Killed Oller at Flat Woods.—Robbed Bean's store at Irondale.

About the middle of August, 1863, at the solicitation of two brave boys who had kindly assisted me on several trips to St. Francois county, and expected my assistance in return, I started to a small place called Hamburg, with fifteen men under my command.

We wished to take in three or four Dutchmen who had given the relatives of my two men a great deal of trouble, causing them to be robbed, and in some instances imprisoned.

We crossed into Butler county, and then into Stoddard; passing south and east of Bloomfield, we crossed Little river above Buffington, and entered Scott county. By traveling altogether in the night we created no disturbance until we got near the point to which we were aiming.

About ten o'clock in the forenoon we rode up and surrounded the house of one of the men whom we were after. He recognized us as Union soldiers and came out without being called. He commenced addressing us in Dutch, but I told him that we did not belong to that persuasion; he then began speaking broken English and still advanced toward us. When in the act of extending his hand toward one of my men who was nearest to him, he suddenly discovered his unfortunate mistake, and called to his wife who was yet in the house. The whole family came out, placed themselves in a group near us and implored us in broken English to spare their father. To the bottom of my heart I cursed the man who first invented war; but as war on one side and mercy on the other would only lead to death, we marched our Dutchman off about a mile and hung him to a leaning tree. About one hour afterwards we came to the house of another of those cunning informers; he broke out at a back door and ran so fast that we all had to fire before we brought him down.

We now pushed on to get a couple more who lived at Hamburg, but on entering the place we were met by a volley of musket shots which made our ears ring. One of my men was killed on the spot, at which we charged the enemy, seeing that their numbers were only about twelve. They took refuge behind an old dilapidated frame house; and while I placed some of my men in positions to command both ends of the building, others marched up to the front of the house and set it on fire.

By this time the shooting had attracted the attention of other Federals in the vicinity, who came to the rescue, and before we were aware of their presence we were nearly surrounded. We made a dash to clear their lines, and in the attempt four of my men were badly wounded, but none of them killed.

I began to think that I had met with more than our match, for as we retreated they followed us in a solid phalanx. Our horses were put to the utmost of their speed, our wounded were left behind, the chase after us was gloriously exciting; we probably gained a little after we had gone about two miles, but they did not by any means give up the chase, for we were not allowed to enjoy anything that had the least resemblance to peace and tranquility, until we had gained Little river and swam across to Coon Island. We lost nearly everything we had except our horses and they were badly injured; some of my men lost their guns, and others lost every bit of fight that they formerly had in them. The Federals made no attempt to cross the river, but left us to brood over the sad result of our rash and inconsiderate adventure. The whole matter looked to me a great deal like a defeat, and I must confess that I viewed it rather in that light; but if it had been the Army of the Potomac they would have called it "a strategic movement—merely a change of base."

We lost one man killed and four wounded, prisoners whom we supposed would be shot. In justice to General Steele, however, I can proudly say that in this case he did us more than justice by retaining our men as prisoners of war and treating them well. Their wounds were healed, and in three months they were exchanged and returned to our Green County Confederacy.

On leaving Coon Island we struck the St. Francis river at Twelve Mile creek, and remained there several days recruiting our horses. Not wishing to be idle, I concluded that while my men and horses were resting, I would take a trip on foot to Flat Woods and pay my respects to George F. Oller, who was so intent on bushwhacking me that he spent most of his time in the woods watching for my appearance on my accustomed routes.

Aside from his many boisterous threats against me he was in the habit of marking out "Old Sam," as he called me, on trees and shooting at the figure at various distances. His vindictive spirit was not manifested against me alone, but even against the children of Southern sympathizers. At one time he went to St. Francis river where some Southern boys were in the habit of bathing, and at the high rock from which they were fond of plunging, he drove some cedar stakes and sharpened the upper ends which were just under the water.

Fortunately when the boys next went there to bathe the water had fallen a few inches, and the ends of the stakes exposed so that the boys discovered them before making the fatal leap. Oller of course did all this for the patriotic motive of subjugating the South; but the result was that the little boys were saved and the country lost.

On arriving in the neighborhood I learned from a very kind German lady whom I happened to meet and who mistook me for a Federal, that the hunt for me was still going on.

I learned also that Oller's zeal for the good of the Union cause was not in the least abated by his many failures to hit my figure which he had cut on a large oak near his house, nor by his failure to kill the innocent children whom he was afraid would be Rebels at some future time.

At night I went and inspected his premises, and before daylight I took my position; but the day passed off and he did not make his appearance. When night came I repaired to the house of a friend, obtained two days' rations, returned to my ambush, and slept until the first peep of day. I was again doomed to disappointment; but on the third day, late in the evening, as I lay brooding over the many failures I had made to inflict justice upon those who were seeking my blood, Mr. Oller made his appearance.

He walked slowly up to the premises with his gun on his shoulders. On getting to a pig pen he got over the fence and commenced marking a pig. I shot him through and hastily left the place; on gaining the top of a small hill a few hundred yards off, I heard the pig squealing, for Mr. Oller had fallen across it, and it was not able to extricate itself from the trap.

On getting back to my men I selected five of them to go with me, and permitted the rest to return to Arkansas.

As soon as it was dark I started with my five men for Irondale, on the St. Louis and Iron Mountain railroad.

Just after dark on one evening in the early part of September, we entered the town. We saw no soldiers in the streets, and no one else, except Dr. Poston, a citizen of the place. We compelled him to knock at the door of Bean's store and ask for admittance; when this was done we entered without any trouble, took all the goods we could conveniently pack, and returned to Arkansas by the way of Black river.

CHAPTER XXI.

Started with six men for Springfield, Missouri.—Deceived by a Federal Spy.—Was captured through mistake by Rebels.—Surprised on Panther creek.—Returned home on foot.

I was under obligations to assist some of my boys in a trip to the neighborhood from which they had been driven, in return for their services on several of my trips.

About the middle of September, after having only rested about a week, I started with six men from near Springfield, Missouri, to make a raid in the vicinity of that city. Not being acquainted with the country over which we designed traveling, I had but little to say in regard to the programme of our intended raid. After our plans were arranged, we started, taking with us "neither purse nor scrip," for we intended to rely altogether on our good fortune for our supplies.

From Green county, Ark., we traveled through Randolph and entered Missouri in Ripley county. Here we were detained, for one of my men had the misfortune to lose his horse. Having reached a part of the country known as the Irish Wilderness, we concluded to rest a day and hunt.

In the evening before we struck camp, a young man, dressed in citizen's clothes, who claimed to be going to the Rebel army, joined us, and asked permission to stop with us until morning. He professed to be going to Arkansas, and we readily consented to entertain him as best we could.

After the confusion incident to striking camp, making fires, attending to our horses, etc., was over, our new companion began a series of interrogatories relative to the part of country through which we had operated, since the beginning of the war. After having posted him thoroughly in regard to the field of our operations, we related to him many thrilling incidents and daring adventures connected with our history; to all of which he listened with intense interest, and at the amusing parts of our story he laughed most heartily. After we grew tired of relating our many dangerous feats and bloody deeds, he began his narrative of hair breadth escapes and heroic adventures. The field of his operations having been Kentucky, we were very pleasantly entertained by receiving the full accounts of several incidents of which we had heard some rumors.

We had scarcely marked the transition from twilight to Egyptian darkness, so much were we pleased with our new companion's pleasant stories, when one of my men remarked that "the last hour of the day was melting away into the eventful past." Our programme for the day following had been made by our new comrade, and heartily approved by us all, that we would take an old fashioned deer hunt, among the wild hills surrounding us.

Our quiet slumbers were scarcely disturbed even by the intermission of rolling over, until "Old Sol" was looking us fair in the face, as if to read the guilt of our hearts.

Upon awakening, one word loudly spoken, was sufficient to bring the whole squad to a half recumbent position; and as we went through the antiquated performance of rubbing our eyes, the attention of each one seemed to be turned to the spot where our new comrade had deposited himself for a sleep a few hours before. He was gone! The fragment of an old log, that had served him as a pillow, was all that was left of him or his bed. But this was not all;—one of our best horses was gone! We cared but little for the horse, so far as his real value was concerned, for we had some experience in "raising horses," and knew that we could get another on very easy terms, but we did not like the idea of having been gulled by a young adventurous loyalist, in the face of the fact, too, that we considered ourselves "shark proof."

Neither were we certain that our misfortunes would end here, for our "sharper" had succeeded in getting our plans for the entire trip.

During the preparation of our morning meal, the subject of our misfortune was freely discussed, with many conjectures in regard to who our deceiver was, and the probable result of his acquired information.

A majority of the men were in favor of continuing our journey, while only one man joined me in opposing any further movement in the direction of Springfield.

However, as it was not my own trip, I did not feel at liberty to say much about it; not wishing to appear obstinate, I contented myself with making them a "humbug" speech, for I must confess that the recollection of our unfortunate adventure at that place, seemed as though it would haunt me to the grave. All my arguments, however, did no good, they would not be convinced against their own will; so I submitted cheerfully to the good old democratic rule of going with the majority.

During the day, myself and two others, rode over to the edge of the settlements to get a horse for our pedestrian "bushwhacker," and succeeded in finding one; but the owner was a noted Rebel; our only way to sustain ourselves in the act was to pass ourselves off for Union soldiers, this we did with a very good grace and got the horse without any resistance. In fact, he made but little objection, for he knew that the "Union savers" were terrible when irritated.

After going back two or three miles toward our camp in the Wilderness, I saw some deer on the side of an adjoining hill, and fearing that the boys in camp had failed to kill meat for our supper, selected a nice buck and shot him dead on the spot.

After having dressed the meat preparatory to carrying it into camp, we concluded to build a fire and broil some of it for our dinner. While we were thus busily engaged, all squatted around the fire, we were suddenly saluted by a remarkably boisterous mandate of "surrender!" at which we sprang to our feet with our revolvers in our hands to find ourselves confronted by five of Capt. Bolin's men, who had left Green county, Arkansas, a few days before us, and were on a visit to see some friends in the neighborhood, from one of whom we had taken the horse. We had anything else rather than a fight, for we quickly recognized each other, and a general congratulation was the only military demonstration between us.

The five "bushwhackers" were concealed near the house of the old Rebel from whom we had taken the horse, and who had really regarded us as Federals. As soon as we had left his house, he reported us to Capt. Bolin's men, who took our trail and tracked us to the wild solitudes of the Irish Wilderness. We at once decided on changing our quarters. I sent my two comrades to the camp and had the boys to move over to the edge of the settlements. The old Rebel, from whom we had taken the horse, was our best friend; we gave it back to him, and got another in that neighborhood on the following night.

The reader, without making any very extravagant draw upon his imagination, can conclude that we had a jolly time when we all got together.

Our adventure with the sharper, my attempt to steal the old Rebel's horse, and our unconditional surrender in the Wilderness while broiling the venison, were the subjects discussed. From the boys, we learned something more of our adventurous Yankee detective. He had been in that neighborhood a week or two, repeating the same story that he had told us. He evidently thought that the bushwhackers were rather thick in that neighborhood, and concluded to leave it as quick as possible.

On the following morning, our whole party, with myself, took up our march for Springfield, and in the evening of the same day we reached the vicinity of Thomasville, in Oregon county. We were warned against traveling in the day time, unless we were hunting for a fight; we assured our friends that a fight was the least of our desire at the present time, the object of our trip being solely for the purpose of enabling some of our boys to avenge certain wrongs received at the hands of Union men in Greene county, Missouri.

After making a tolerable heavy draw on some of our Rebel friends for provisions and horse-feed, we again resumed our journey, and the following morning found us in the woods, quartered for the day, near a small town in Howell county, called Lost Camp, where we remained all day.

A substantial old friend living near by, brought us two or three bottles of "burst-head," which produced the effect of making some of the boys believe that they had fought a great battle, and that the United States Government had taken refuge in a deep cavern, the mouth of which they had stopped with a large flat rock, on top of which the boys were dancing. The only question with them seemed to be what they would do with their twenty millions of prisoners.

When sable night again clad the wicked world in half mourning, we resumed our journey, and on approach of day, we were in the beautiful little town of Vera Cruz, in Douglas county; on the next night we reached Panther creek, in Webster county. One of our men who professed to be acquainted in that neighborhood, went to a pretended Rebel friend to get supplies, but the old fellow flatly refused to give him anything. I was a little amused at the disappointment of the boys, and at the dilemma in which they were placed. I could not help thinking how different I would have acted on a raid of my own.

About ten o'clock in the forenoon we were surprised by a party of Federal soldiers, numbering perhaps about sixty men. Before we were aware of their presence they charged upon us at a most furious rate, yelling and shooting at us most fearfully. A mere glance at the party was sufficient to convince me that an attempt at resistance would be worse than folly. I sprang to my feet, yelled out to the boys to run; but having no time to mount our horses, we had to depend upon our own fleetness for our escape. In our retreat through the dense forest, we had the advantage over our enemies; I and four others managed to keep together for about a mile; not seeing any pursuers, we took our position on a high hill, and remained there until late in the evening. While keeping a vigilant watch over the surrounding country, we discovered one of our men emerging cautiously from a dense thicket in the valley at the foot of the hill.

He seemed terribly frightened. I made my way down the hill to within a hundred yards of him, and then called him by name; but it was some time before he recognized me. Fortunately for us, this man was acquainted with the country through which we would have to pass in making our way back to Arkansas. The tops of the highest hills were yet basking in the sun's last lingering rays, when we started on our perilous journey of two hundred miles on foot, without any blankets, provisions, or anything else, except our pistols and one gun, for I had made my escape with old "Kill-devil" in my hand. The next morning about daylight, we ran into a gang of sheep, succeeded in catching one, and made our way down into a deep ravine, where we could not be discovered. There we built a fire and fared sumptuously. We continued on during the night, and the next day I killed a deer. On the following night we reached our friend near Vera Cruz, and here we met another one of our boys, but he was no better posted in regard to the fate of our company than myself.

I will not weary the patience of my reader by detailing the many privations incident to our trip; suffice it to say that we did get back to Arkansas; and that fortunately for me I never received an invitation to take another trip to Springfield under the command of an unexperienced leather-head.

About a week after arriving in camp, another one of the boys came in, looking somewhat subjugated. I afterwards learned that two of our men were killed when we were routed, and that the others were taken prisoners, none of whom ever returned during the war.

I have cautioned the boys never again to imagine themselves dancing on the flat rock covering the prison door of the defunct Yankee nation, lest they might unexpectedly find some of them yet running at large.

CHAPTER XXII.

Started with four men.—Surrounded in a thicket near Fredericktown.—Escaped with the loss of three horses.—Stole horses
from the Federals at night.—Killed two Federal Soldiers.—Suffered from hunger.—Killed Fowler.—Got a horse from G. W.
Murphy.—Went to Mingo Swamp.—Killed Coots for betraying
him.—Killed a soldier and lost two men.

I selected four good men and started on another trip to St. Francois county,
Missouri, on the 10th of November. We traveled altogether in the night; arriving in
the vicinity of Fredericktown about midnight, we stopped at the house of a well-
known friend, who expressed a great deal of surprise at seeing us there, stating
that the cry of "Hildebrand," had been raised in the community about ten days
previous, and that the Federals, with the assistance of citizens, had been scouting
the woods between that place and Farmington ever since. He was no little amused
when we told him that the report was utterly false, and that we were on a scout
out westward at the time.

The report of my having been in that part of the country ten days previous, I
was satisfied would work favorably to the success of our present enterprise, for it
was not probable that they would make another search so soon after having made
one so thoroughly.

From there we went to a dense thicket near the residence of Mr. North, and
being very tired and sleepy, we lay down, and slept very soundly until the morning sun was looking down upon our quiet retreat. Our old friend had supplied us
with two days' rations and some shelled corn for our horses, so we had a complete
outfit for a good rest.

Whilst lying lazily around our horses, planning the future of our trip, we were
suddenly startled by the sound of a gun near by, which was evidently discharged
at one of us. A moment, however, was sufficient to satisfy me in regard to the
nature of the case; we had been spied out, our horses tracked up, and our thicket
surrounded. At a bound I lit in my saddle and was soon out of the thicket in an
opposite direction from where the gun was fired. On reaching the open ground, I
discovered the Federals coming around the woods, not having yet completed their
circle. They fired on me, but the distance was too great, and I remained unhurt. My
men had not taken time to mount their horses, but as they followed me on foot,
one of them received a bruise on his back from a spent ball. In a few minutes our
complete escape was effected, with no damage but the loss of four good horses.
The Federals followed us closely for about a mile, when we got far enough ahead

to give them the dodge by turning at right angles into the St. Francis river bottom. We made our way back to within a mile of Fredericktown, where we remained the rest of the day. When night came we went in quest of our pursuers; we found them camped in a lane about six miles northwest from Fredericktown.

Our object now was to get horses. We made our way on foot toward them, but found that the end of the lane was guarded; we went around to the other end and found it guarded also, while the horses were in the middle, tied to one of the fences. We then went around through the field, laying down the outside fence very carefully, and approached the lane fence on the opposite side from where the horses were tied. The night was very dark, but we could distinctly see a sentinel slowly walking his beat of about fifty yards, ourselves being at the end of the beat. When his back was turned, I laid the fence down easily; we sprang to a horse a piece, cut the halters, mounted, and were off at full speed before he turned on the other end of his beat.

Our hasty flight of course raised an alarm in the camp, but we saw no more of the Federals that night. Being again mounted, we resolved to give them employment for a few days in hunting us, and for that purpose we took up our quarters in a place least expected, by going within a mile of Fredericktown onto a certain eminence, after having made a circuit around the side of a hill.

On the following day we slept by turns; I killed a pig with my knife near the house of a farmer, and cooked it in a deep ravine where the fire could not be observed; during the previous night we had stolen a sufficiency of feed for our horses. I concluded to go into Fredericktown to get a supply of ammunition, which I did about ten o'clock in the night, by meeting with an old friend there who bountifully supplied us with all we needed.

We moved seven or eight miles in the direction of Pilot Knob, supplying ourselves with horse-feed and provisions on the move.

When morning again made its appearance, I left my men in charge of the horses, and after instructing them where to meet me again in case of trouble, I went to the gravel road for the purpose of killing a Federal or two. I concealed myself near the road, and about 10 o'clock in the day, two came along and I let old "Kill-devil" off at one of them. They wheeled suddenly around and started back in the direction of Pilot Knob; the one I shot was badly wounded and bled freely. Only an hour afterwards a squad of perhaps ten came from the direction of Fredericktown. It was a quandary in my mind whether it was best to take a pop at them or not, a feeling of revenge settled the matter. I fired, and one fell; at this they put their horses to full speed. Soon after they were out of sight, another came along in a very great hurry as if he was endeavoring to overtake the others; on coming up to the dead man he made a momentary halt, of which I took advantage and shot him through. I now concluded that I had done enough for the day, or enough, at least, to raise an excitement, so I went back to my men and we moved about twelve miles in the direction of Farmington, and near the St. Francis river on a high bluff, which afforded us peculiar advantages in the event of a fight, where we were compelled to remain several days.

My comrade, who had received a bruise on the spine, had by this time become so disabled by that slight injury, that he could not ride. The little amusement that I had taken on the gravel road was now creating quite a stir in military circles, and their search for us was carried on with a zeal worthy of a better cause.

Having called out the forces at Pilot Knob, Fredericktown and Farmington, with a large majority of the citizens, the search was made thoroughly and in earnest. Squads frequently passed in sight of us, and within easy gun-shot, but none of them ascended the high bluff we occupied. On the evening of the third day our provisions and horse-feed gave out, and each night I went out in search of more. Obtaining provender for our horses was a very easy matter, but getting provisions for ourselves was not only very difficult but extremely dangerous. I knew but few men in the neighborhood, and on approaching their houses I invariably found our well-known signal of danger—a towel hung on a nail outside of the door. We could easily have killed a hog or a sheep, but we could not run the risk of making a fire to cook it. After our provisions gave entirely out, we were twenty-four hours without any food. During the second night I found some bacon in somebody's smoke-house, I knew not whether he was a friend or foe, and cared still less, but I took two hams to camp, which we ate raw.

On the sixth night our comrade was able to ride, and we moved about fifteen miles, stopping south of Fredericktown. Here a friend supplied us with the necessaries of life, and even brought food to our camp ready cooked for our use.

Our wounded companion, who was too much disabled to take any part in a raid, now obtained leave to return to Arkansas alone, while I and my other men started on a trip to St. Francois county.

While living at Flat Woods, I became acquainted with a man named John Fowler. He professed to be a strong Southern man, and having perfect confidence in his veracity, I entrusted him with many things in regard to my plans, that I withheld from the rest of my neighbors; but about the time that I was run off from there by the Federals, my friend Fowler joined the Union army.

On receiving this intelligence, I felt much mortified, and concluded at once that he had betrayed me, notwithstanding he sent me word on several occasions that I need not fear him. His duplicity, however, was so apparent that I determined to kill him on sight; this I had some hope of doing, as he seemed to enjoy some liberties, and often came into the neighborhood, but generally in company with other soldiers. On every visit he came to my house and conversed pleasantly with my wife, but I regarded him rather as a spy.

As we were traveling along on the present occasion, I run suddenly on him about five miles southwest from Fredericktown. We met in a narrow path, and before he hardly had time to recognize me, I shot and killed him instantly.

I will here state that I had cause to regret this act afterwards, for I ascertained that he had deserted the Federals, and was on his way South to join the "bushwhacking department" of the Southern army.

After passing Fredericktown in the night, we learned that several companies of Federals, Home Guards and Militia, were hunting for me in every direction. In fact, we came near being discovered by several squads during the night. We hastened on into St. Francois county; Tom Haile and myself being in front, we took Farmington without firing a gun long before my other men came up. As we rode in the streets were full of people, but we only had time to take a second look when the place seemed to be entirely deserted. Not a man, woman or child could be found, at which Tom laughed heartily, and remarked that he thought cellar rent ought to be very high in that place. When my other men came up Tom told them that we had found a beautiful town not claimed by anybody, "just laying around loose," and that he was very sorry we could not take it along with us until we found an owner. We did not haunt the town very long with our unholy presence, but after going into a grocery, where we had to help ourselves, we took a hearty drink of some good old liquor that had been left by the generation that once lived there; then mounting our horses we left the lonesome place. Tom remarked that as we had no wounded man to leave there to garrison the town we had better leave for the "settlements." We went on to Big river to look after our old enemies; but their consciousness of having committed such a catalogue of crimes against me made them the hardest men in the world to find.

In our business of killing enemies, we met with good success everywhere but on Big river. Up to the time of the present writing, a majority of those miscreants, with hands dripping with the blood of my brothers, are yet permitted to live. For several days and nights we watched around the houses of my old enemies, but to no purpose; it was impossible to find them. One of my men made his way around through the neighborhood to ascertain their whereabouts, and reported that they were all from home except Franklin Murphy; but Tom Haile was determined that I should not kill him. He exacted a promise from me long ago that I never would molest him or any of his property. Haile was a man who wielded an influence over every one with whom he came in contact. He was ever in a perfect good humor; the clouds of adversity never seemed to throw a shadow on his brow; his heart was all sunshine, and his feet ever trod in the vales of mirth and gladness.

I plainly saw that so far as killing my old enemies was concerned my present trip was a failure. During all the incidents of my previous trips to Missouri, I never for once lost sight of that one leading object of my mind. The killing of Federals, in which I had taken such an active part, only afforded me pleasure by the reflection that they were a part and parcel of the same stripe, and in sympathy with the Big river vigilance mob.

I was now much in need of a good horse, and after talking the matter over with my men, Tom Haile and myself concluded to demand a good horse, bridle and saddle, from G. W. Murphy, a man whose nature it was to be quiet and inoffensive, and who had attended strictly to his own business during all the struggle.

He was abundantly able to assist us in the matter, and we considered that he ought to contribute that much toward the Southern cause. We were raised close together from boyhood, and I had nothing against him; but as he was well able to spare me a horse, I made the demand. He complied with the request after emerging (as I believe) from a barrel of feathers. His novel appearance caused Tom Haile, who was always fond of a joke, to tell him that he must not let Jim Craig see him in that condition, or he might capture him for a spotted mule, which Murphy, in his good humored way, passed off very well. We also took a horse from Orville McIlvaine, who lived on the place known as the Baker farm. I had some anxiety to see him in order to make him break his well-known rule of never parting with a greenback after it got into his safe; but his retiring nature prompted him to conceal himself in the garret until we departed. We now rejoined the other boys and started back by the way of Mingo Swamp. Before we reached that place we were warned by our friends that the Federals were thick in that locality. About midnight we arrived at the house of William Coots (well-known as old Bill Coots,) who had heretofore invariably represented himself as a Rebel of unusual bitterness. In answer to our inquiries, he told us that there were no Federals in the neighborhood, neither had there been any for more than a month. He also told us that the men we wished to find were then at home. I felt very much gratified on hearing statements so favorable to the success of our enterprise, and requested him to supply us with a few days' rations and provender for our horses, while we camped at a certain point not more than half a mile distant.

He readily consented, and gave us a very pressing invitation to come and take breakfast with him about sun up. To this we agreed, and at the time designated, we all left our camp and repaired to the house of our generous host, who received us with a great deal of what might be termed "Arkansas courtesy." It may be readily supposed that the scanty fattening process we had gone through while on the St. Francis bluff had produced a streak of lean running the whole length of our mortal bodies; and that the odor from the kitchen, of coffee, ham and eggs, with other ingredients intermixed with spices, made us for a time forget all other things on these mundane shores. When breakfast was announced and we were about to seat ourselves at the table, old Coots remarked: "Here, gentlemen, you can lay your arms on the bed," but it was not our custom to take off our arms at any time, so we seated ourselves at the table with them on. We were perhaps about half done eating when a ragged looking Federal stepped up to the door, and in an exulting tone said: "Well, Coots! you got them, did you?" and bawled out "surrender," at which I sprang from the table, drew my revolver and shot Coots, seized my gun which I had left near the door, and cleared the door by about fifteen feet; I shot a Federal with my revolver which I still held in my right hand, and in a few bounds gained the woods unhurt, save a slight wound on the back of my head. My men attempted to follow without their guns, two of them were killed in their attempt to escape, while the remaining one (Tom Haile,) soon got with me, and we made our way to our horses. Fortunately the Federals had not found them. We tarried awhile for our comrades, but as they did not come up we were fearful that they were slain. Mounting our horses and leading theirs, we made our way to a canebrake about a mile off, and sent a citizen back to ascertain the real state of affairs. After taking an old bridle in his hand, he made his way over, inquiring of each person he met for a grey mare and a black colt.

On passing the house of old Bill Coots he was halted, at which he did not seem to be the least alarmed, but expressed the utmost surprise when the whole tragedy was related to him. The worst part of the whole affair was that two of my men were killed and were lying at the time in front of the house. On receiving this news we started home to get a force sufficient to clean out the Federals, but on arriving in Green county, Arkansas, nearly all of our men were out on scouting excursions, principally toward the West.

SAM HILDEBRAND BETRAYED BY COOTS.

CHAPTER XXIII.

Took ten men.—Went to Mingo Swamp.—Went to Castor Creek.—
Medicine traffic.—Attacked two companies of Federals under
Capt. Cawhorn and Capt. Rhoder.—Fought them seven nights.—
Dick Cowan.—Went with Capt. Reed's men.—Attacked Capt.
Leeper's Company.—Killed fourteen and wounded eight.—Cap-
tured forty-four guns, sixty pistols, forty horses and four hundred
dollars.

On the 15th day of December, 1863, I started back to Mingo Swamp with ten
men, and met with no obstacles on our route after swimming the St. Francis river.
When we got into the neighborhood of the unfortunate tragedy of our previous
trip, we ascertained from reliable sources that the Federals left for Bloomfield on
the day following the skirmish at old Bill Coots', and that the men we had been
looking after so long had gone into the regular army.

We visited the house of our newly made widow, Mrs. Coots, for the purpose
of seeing the graves of my two brave boys. She confessed that Coots had layed
plans for my capture; that the Federals were camped only one mile off at the time,
and that after I had consented to come to his house for breakfast, he went to the
Federal camp and notified them of the fact, and made arrangements to take me
in. Finding no one in that vicinity to fight, we made our way over onto Castor
creek to a well known friend, who had, since the beginning of the war, acted as an
agent for us in receiving and forwarding supplies and medicines. Hearing of no
Federals in that portion of the country, and there being no persons in that quarter
against whom we had enmity sufficient to induce us to invest any of our capital in
bark or grape vines, we obtained the medicine sent to that place from Farmington,
St. Francois county, Missouri, and started back for Mingo Swamp. On our way
the monotony of our journey was suddenly relieved by seeing a Federal coming
toward us, apparently riding very cautiously. We only got a glimpse of him as the
road took him down into a small ravine out of our sight. We were very certain that
he had not discovered us, so we got out of the road until he came up; when we
halted him he seemed very much frightened, but surrendered quietly.

He told us that he had been to Cairo, Illinois, to see his family, and was on his
way back to his command at Fredericktown. Upon the whole he gave such a good
account of himself that we only disarmed him and took his greenbacks, which,
however, only amounted to twelve dollars.

On the following night we heard of three more Rebel boys in the country and
sent for them. After they agreed to try a trip with us, we left the drugs with a

friend and went back onto Castor creek to watch for the Federals who were in the habit of passing there on their road between Fredericktown and Cape Girardeau. We had been there but one night and day when we heard of two companies of Federals nearby commanded by Captains Cawhorn and Rhoder. As soon as it was dark we proceeded to spy out their exact locality and take a look at the surroundings. We found from their position and numbers that it would be entirely unsafe to charge through their camp as was our custom, and concluded to bushwhack them. During the night we killed twelve and wounded several more, as we were informed afterwards. When day again made its appearance we went about two miles into a dense thicket with our horses. We put out spies watching and waiting impatiently for them to move. Instead of marching, however, they were charging around the most public places in the vicinity, threatening Southern sympathizers with annihilation, but we got no chance to bushwhack them.

During the day a squad of them went to the residence of Dick Cowan, one of my men, burned his house and other buildings, and attempted an outrage on one of his sisters who happened to be there. For several days the people in the neighborhood were compelled to suffer the most glaring insults and wrongs. Each night we renewed the attack, and killed one occasionally at all hours of the night. They stood our mode of warfare six days and nights, but early on the morning of the seventh day they started on their way to Cape Girardeau. During their march we stationed ourselves at convenient places, and as they came along poured a deadly fire into their ranks and then retreated into the woods. We thought by this means to induce them to follow us, but it only seemed to hurry up their march. This we repeated three times before they reached Cape Girardeau.

By this time we were anxious to see our families and started back to Arkansas. Taking our drugs that had been left with a friend, we soon met twenty-eight of Capt. Reed's men who insisted on our taking a trip with them to Wayne county, and perhaps as far north as Iron county. To this I consented, detailing two of my men to take the drugs to Arkansas, we started on our way, marching in day time. We passed about twenty miles south of Bloomfield and on to Greenville, in Wayne county, arriving there about sunset, but did not find any Federal troops in the place to protect its loyalty. Soon after arriving in town we heard of a company of Federals on Lost creek under Capt. Leeper, and taking our informant for a guide we marched at once to give them a fight.

Reaching there about sunrise the next morning we charged their camp, running their pickets in at full speed, fought them only a few minutes, when those who had not got into the brush surrendered. In the fight we lost four men killed and six wounded, the latter, however, all recovered. Of the enemy we killed fifteen, wounded eight, and took ten prisoners beside the wounded. Our booty consisted of forty-four guns, sixty pistols, forty horses, four hundred dollars in greenbacks, and other articles of value to us and to our families.

The subject of what disposition we would make of the prisoners came up, and in cases of the kind we were purely democratic, so we took the vote whether we would kill them or set them loose.

In consideration of the wrongs my family had received at their hands, and of their well-known cruelty, I made a speech in favor of killing them and voted accordingly.

When the whole vote was counted I found myself in the minority by just two votes; but true to my word I released them, unarmed and on foot.

In the evening before we had attacked them they had killed an old man by the name of Tom McKee and burned his house with other buildings. This fresh outrage was not known to us until they were gone, or we undoubtedly would have shot them. On being informed of this fact, however, we sent a scout after them, but they had left the main road and secreted themselves in the thick woods. The wounded, however, were at our disposal, but we did not, during the whole war get mean enough to imitate our enemies by killing wounded prisoners, but placed them at the house of a widow woman who promised to take care of them until the Federals at Pilot Knob could have them removed.

We procured a wagon and loaded it with our booty; took our six wounded men and started back to Green county, Arkansas, where we arrived without any difficulty, and found all things right at headquarters.

CHAPTER XXIV.

Took fifteen men. Captured three Federals. Hung one. Captured a squad of Federals. Reception of "Uncle Bill." Hung all the prisoners. Captured five more, and hung one.

After spending the winter very agreeably, on the 10th day of March, 1864, I concluded to make a raid to the vicinity of Jackson, Cape Girardeau county, Missouri, with fifteen men, several of whom were from that county, and knew the people and country well.

It was to remunerate these men for the invaluable services they had rendered me on several of my trips that I consented to go with them.

We passed through Butler county into Stoddard, leaving Bloomfield to the south a few miles, crossed the southeast corner of Bollinger and into Cape Girardeau.

Having traveled very slowly, and altogether in the night, we had created no disturbance on our way, nor interfered with any one, for it was our custom to make no demonstrations until we were ready to return.

In the latter part of the night we arrived in the vicinity of Jackson, selected a good place and camped for the day, during which time some of the boys visited their friends. One of my men who was an entire stranger in that part of the country, went into the town to get whisky, and to see what was going on.

On returning late in the evening he told me that there were three Federals in town who seemed to be well acquainted with the people, and that they were behaving very well. He wanted to take some of the boys and go back after them, to which I consented. They started off in eager haste, but soon returned with the three prisoners, having met them in the road some distance from town. Not knowing them I retained them as prisoners until the boys came in who knew them. Being governed by their statements, I released two of the Federals and kept the other as a prisoner, and took him with us when we started that night for White Water, but we did not take him far before we tied him to a limb.

On White Water we remained inactive several days, receiving the kindest treatment from our Southern friends, which enabled some of my men to visit their friends and relatives.

About sunset one evening a citizen came to us and stated that about an hour before nine Federals had passed the road, and the probabilities were that they would stop for the night at the first house.

The night was now growing very dark, and we were soon under full pursuit of them. On nearing the house, however, we rode very slowly, and tied our horses in the thicket at some distance, and approached the premises very cautiously. It was a double hewed log house, with an open hall between them, with a small cooking apartment forming an ell to the main building, but separated from it by a narrow hall also.

After forming my men in a line around the house I crept to the windows and peeped into both rooms, only one of which, however, was lighted, and in it I could see no one except a very old lady, who might have been a grandmother, and some little children who were grouped around the old lady, and who seemed to be holding a very earnest conversation with her in a very low tone. I went around to the kitchen window, and upon looking in to my great joy I saw the Federals eating their supper.

The position I occupied was a very easy one, and their conversation was so peculiarly interesting that I could not refrain from listening. They were using very vulgar and indecent language to the lady, who, with all the kindness and amiability characteristic of her sex, was waiting upon the ruffians, while the old gentleman was seated on a box in a corner of the room exposed to the most outrageous insults, accompanied with threats of the most heinous character; but in silent fear the old man bore their criminal epithets and bitter curses without returning a word.

By this time I had heard all that my weak humanity could bear. I retreated from my position, passed around the circle, and collected my men at the entrance to the kitchen into the open hall, this being their only place of egress, and placed an equal number of my men on each side. I now stepped into the door and demanded a surrender, at which my men became impatient and rushed for the door, but I prevented them from entering. Each of the Federals pushed back his chair, at which I told them that I would shoot any man who should attempt to arise from the table with his arms, admitting my men at the same time. At this the Federals placed their revolvers on the table and retired according to my command to the fartherest end of the room and formed in a line.

By this time our little disturbance had aroused the old grandmother and the little children in the other house, who came to the scene, the children screaming in a terrible manner, and clinging to the old lady's dress for protection. On reaching the kitchen, however, the scene was quite different from what they had expected. They halted a moment at the door in dreadful suspense, then suddenly the oldest girl, who was about eight years of age, sprang suddenly into the room, exclaiming "Well, grandma! if here ain't Uncle Bill!" then seizing one of my men by the hand she sobbed aloud, "Oh Uncle Bill! don't let the soldiers kill pa!" at which the whole household greeted "Uncle Bill." The old gentleman last of all approached my man who had been recognized and greeted with so many smiles and such marked distinction, giving his hand slowly while the tears trickled down his weather-beaten cheek, and only said: "Bill, I'm glad to see you," my comrade receiving his hand and retaining it for perhaps half a minute, said nothing, but turned and introduced me as Major Hildebrand to his relative, and to the household. As I stepped forward to receive the salutation of the old gentleman of whom I had heard so much, and knew so little, I heard one of the prisoners remark, "a hell of a Major," and upon casting my eyes around I found them ready to burst into a derisive laughter, which I must confess took me a little back.

At this I ordered one of the rooms forming the main building lighted, and stationing my men properly, I marched my prisoners out of the kitchen through the little hall into the room of the main building, put a guard over them and pickets around the house, I returned to the kitchen with my man now known as "Uncle Bill," to have a talk with the old gentleman while his wife was hastily preparing a nice little supper for us all. The old man again took me by the hand, thanking me for my coincidental visit, stated that the Federals had made several trips into the neighborhood after him, but having been told of their threats, he had always heretofore succeeded in eluding their search. He also stated that the only charge they had against him was for feeding bushwhackers, and that when the soldiers came up to his house on the present occasion, just after dark, they were in the hall before he saw them, and he had no possible way of escape except through them.

Considering his escape so very uncertain, he resolved to submit to his fate, and that when we made our timely appearance he was a prisoner, sentenced to be executed as soon as they were done supper. He wound up his statement by saying: "Well, Major Hildebrand, I must confess I am very agreeably disappointed in your general appearance; I have long been anxious to see you, and am surprised that you never called on me before, but if you had done so I should never have taken you for Sam Hildebrand. I was led to believe, by hearing of your exploits, that you certainly was a rough looking customer, a perfect "raw-head and bloody-bones;" and that Beelzebub himself would have been daunted by your ferocious appearance."

Supper being announced eight men were left to guard the prisoners while the others were eating, until all had partaken of the sumptuous repast. We were now ready for business, we marched our prisoners out to the fence in front of the house, tied their hands securely behind them, placed them on their own horses and tied their feet together underneath. Then mounting we started south, leading the horses on which the prisoners rode. Having traveled very fast we reached a part of the country as day began to approach in which we felt perfectly safe.

Leaving the road we went into a deep ravine about fifteen miles northeast from Bloomfield, covered with thick undergrowth and sheltered by heavy timber. Here we hung our prisoners. They were really brave fellows, and submitted to their fate without a murmur, and during our march that night they showed not the least sign of being conquered, but said they were McNeal's men, and that when they went into the army it was for the purpose of killing Rebels, and that some of the worst Rebels they had killed were men who were staying at home, and the most of them professing to be "loyal."

After disposing of our prisoners, we secreted our horses in a dense thicket, and ten of us took our stations on a road leading from Benton, Scott county, Missouri, to watch for Federals. We remained here nearly all day without seeing any, and were thinking about giving it up as a bad job and returning to our camps; but when the sun was about an hour high, in the evening, we discovered five Federals wending their way slowly toward Bloomfield.

My men were divided into two parties, and were stationed about one hundred yards apart. We allowed them to get nearly opposite the second squad of which I was one, then we stepped suddenly into the road before them and demanded a surrender, to which they submitted, but seemed very much alarmed. On calling up my men who had been stationed farther down the road, and who stood at this time behind the prisoners. They seemed somewhat relieved as they recognized one of them as being an old acquaintance, who extended his hand cordially to all of them but one, remarking to him that he would not shake hands with him "until he met him in h—ll."

They now dismounted and surrendered up their arms and their horses. I then marched them out of the road to a safe distance into the woods and inquired of my man who had recognized them, concerning their character. He reported that all of them were his acquaintances of long standing; that four of them were very clever fellows, these I released immediately; but the fifth one we hung after investigating his case.

When night came we mounted our horses, and taking our booty with us, started back to Arkansas.

CHAPTER XXV.

As we all belonged to the "Independent Bushwhacking Department of the Confederate States of America," and were entirely dependent on our own exertions for a livelihood, it was necessary now that we should put in our crops.

For nearly two months Crowley's Ridge on which we lived, and the adjacent country, looked as if it contained an industrious little community of "honest farmers."

The axe was heard in every direction; the smoke from burning brush was curling up from a thousand fires, and at night the little boys and girls were making bright fires until midnight, under the impression hinted at by their fathers that it was "such fun." All day long the women were out in full force with their hoes and their rakes, unmindful of the music of crying babies heard at nearly every cabin. Mothers are nearly always deaf while planting out onions; it is a little season of orphanage through which most children in the country have to pass once a year. We have all passed through that bitter day with red eyes, and it is no wonder that the sight of an onion in after life is so apt to bring tears in our eyes.

I put in a good crop of corn, and my wife made an excellent garden with no help but the children. I am very much tempted to brag a little on my excellent wife, but if I were to assert that I had the best wife in the world, each one of my male readers who are married would want me to except his own; this would render the exceptions so numerous that my wife would come in nearly last, so I will say nothing about it, and keep my own opinion to myself.

After plowing my crop over once I made preparation for another trip to Missouri, but we had all got into such a good humor while busily engaged in farming, that we were nearly two days recounting our grievances before we were mad enough to think of snatching our enemies into eternity.

Taking nine men, one of whom had served under Quantrel, we started on the 25th day of May, 1864, for another raid into Missouri. Crossing the St. Francis river at the southwest corner of Stoddard county, we went into Scott county and watched three days and nights to catch some men we were after, but failing in this we went in the direction of Dallas, the county seat of Bollinger.

My men wanted to return, as nothing of an exciting interest had transpired so far; but at my earnest solicitation they agreed to go with me one more day. The next morning we were traveling in day time, and had not proceeded more than four or five miles when we discovered a party of Federals, seven in number, who had discovered us and were under full speed toward the town of Dallas, which was at that time garrisoned by about one hundred Dutch soldiers. We dashed on after them; the race was a very exciting one. When we had gone about six miles we began to gain on them, and when we got within a mile of the garrison one of their horses fell, giving the rider a thump on the ground that knocked him senseless until we were upon him. We disarmed him, and as his horse had not left, we made him mount and go with us about two miles in the woods.

The Dutchman seemed very much alarmed, and gave us enough broken English for a good sized volume; but as soon as we arrived in a thick timbered hollow between the hills, we quietly sent his spirit back to the Rhine where it never should have left. In a few hours we called at the house of a friend, fed our horses and got some refreshments for ourselves.

To the Flat Woods, in St. Francois county, we then made our way, and remained there about twenty-four hours, after which we went to the extreme northern part of the county, and concealed ourselves among the Pike Run hills. Those hills are perhaps the most rugged part of the whole State, and are covered with a dense thicket of underbrush, making it a wild, uninhabited wilderness. These hills not being far from Big river, they afforded me a secure place for my temporary headquarters while searching around for my enemies.

Early in the morning I engaged the services of a well known friend, who feigned business in several parts of the neighborhood, who returned at night and reported that only two of my persecutors were at home, whose name were James Walls and John Baker.

On the following morning when the light of day again pierced through the gloom of our retreat I went and stationed myself near the house where they both resided.

I did not watch long before Walls came out onto the porch. But I had failed to get a position sufficiently near for me to kill him at the house; I was watching for them to come to the wood pile, which would only have been about one hundred yards. I could always hit a spot as large as a man's hand at that distance with old "Kill-devil."

About ten o'clock two men rode up to the house, alighted and went in; they came out again in half an hour followed by both Walls and Baker, who started off in an opposite direction from where I lay. I then changed my position to the opposite side of the house, thinking they probably would return soon.

I remained quietly until the sun had dipped behind the western hills, then I returned to camp where I again found my friend who had acted as a spy for me. He told me that he had seen Baker and Walls going in the direction of De Soto with two other men, one of whom stated to him that "Sam Hildebrand was thought to be in the country, from the fact that strange and very rough looking men had been seen at several public places, and that they were thought to be Hildebrand's men."

The reader will here understand that these unwarrantable scares were very frequent in this vicinity; one poor ragged stranger making his appearance in the neighborhood was sufficient at any time to raise the cry of "Hildebrand," at which all who had wronged me would squat like young quails.

Knowing that any further efforts to kill either Walls or Baker would be fruitless, I concluded to run the risk of watching the town of Big River Mills, which was at that time a place of rendezvous for the Militia, where they generally collected before starting out against me.

I accordingly took my station on a bluff overlooking the main road leading from the settlement of my old enemies to that place, being about a quarter of a mile below the town and fifty yards from the road. At daylight I was on the bluff and ready for business. During the day people passed the road at intervals of from fifteen minutes to half an hour; but none of them were the men I wanted to kill. From the position I occupied I could easily recognize the features of any one with whom I was formerly acquainted.

In the evening, about an hour by sun, I discovered a man riding slowly and alone toward the town, whom I recognized as Joe McGahan. A thrill of intense satisfaction pervaded my whole system, which it would be folly in me to attempt to describe. The English language from its high standard of dignity to its inexhaustible mine of scathing invective would be inadequate to describe the supreme contempt I felt for that man. When I reflected that one of the men who had dipped his hands in the blood of my brothers was now within the range of my gun, my feelings of joy, mingled with a hope of success was indescribable. Nearer and nearer he came, unconscious that retributive justice was hanging over his head; and as he approached the desired point I raised my trusty rifle to my face, placed my finger on the trigger, and was nearly in the act of pulling when the man turned his face a little toward me, when I discovered the sad and almost fatal mistake, that instead of being McGahan it was a man by the name of Sharp. He was a Union man living near by, but was a worthy man and highly esteemed by all who knew him. I almost involuntarily hailed him in order to explain and apologize, but was checked instantly by the return of reason. As he passed slowly out of sight my eyes were riveted on him until a point of the bluff around which he had passed broke the spell. I was deeply absorbed in thought, and the question naturally arose in my mind, why I should have been so often thwarted in my attempts to mete out justice to one who was a scourge to the land that gave him birth, and who had not even the magnanimity of the rattlesnake whose alarm is heard before the blow is struck.

I arrived finally to the conclusion that his Satanic Majesty, who still ruled the infernal regions without a rival, was jealous of his protege upon earth where he still needed his services, and that he wished to delay the period when he would be compelled to doff his crown to a superior.

I did not remain long in ambush after I had come so near committing a terrible error; but hastened through the woods, back to my retreat among the Pike Run hills, and found my men awaiting my return with anxious impatience. As soon as it was dark we started south, and after midnight reached the pinery, southwest from Farmington, and slept there until late in the morning. Our horses were much fagged, we saw that it was best to swap them off before proceeding on our journey.

During the day we stationed ourselves near the plank road between Farmington and Pilot Knob, to watch for an opportunity of exchanging horses. A large company of Federals passed by, but they were too numerous for our purpose. Toward evening we saw three men approaching who were mounted upon fine looking horses. The names of the men were Burges, Hughes and Kelley. We lost no time in capturing the party, and to prevent them from reporting us too soon, we made them go with us several miles over the rugged hills and deep ravines.

Not understanding this movement, they seemed much alarmed, thinking probably that we designed "barking" them.

Old man Burges begged manfully for his life, and shed an occasional tear; but I told him that as they were not Federal soldiers, and that as I had no personal animosity against them, it would be barbarous in the extreme for us to harm them. We took their horses, gave them our own and then released them. They left seemingly very well pleased with the arrangement, and as we had rather out-jockeyed them, we certainly had no right to complain.

We kept near the road leading to Pilot Knob until near sunset, when we came to Abright's store. Abright was a good Union Dutchman, and was not in the habit of crediting bushwhackers, so we robbed his store of all we wanted and then taking the woods we changed our course.

Night soon overtook us, and we traveled eastward until we got into the neighborhood where Mr. Bess resided, on White Water. It was now late in the morning, and we took our position on the top of a high hill where we had a fine view of the surrounding country, and especially of the main road along which the Federals were in the habit of passing from Cape Girardeau to Fredericktown.

In the evening, while most of us were sleeping, my pickets discovered a small squad of soldiers about half a mile off, making their way westward. On being awakened I directed my men to follow me, went down to the road which was skirted by very thick undergrowth, where we secreted ourselves in two parties about fifty yards apart, giving orders not to fire on the Federals unless they showed fight or attempted to run. When they got near the second squad we stepped out into the road and demanded them to surrender. Our appearance was so sudden that they had no time to draw their weapons. Several of them wheeled their horses for a run, but on discovering themselves faced on that side also they threw up their hands in token of a willingness to surrender.

I made them dismount and stack their arms against a tree; after which we marched them into the woods to where our horses were and proceeded to question them.

Then I told them who I was, at which they seemed rather pleased, and remarked that they had often heard of me, and although they had no desire to fall into my hands as prisoners of war, yet they always wished to see me.

I asked them if they had not heard of me as being a bushwhacker and withal a very bad man, and that I was in the habit of killing all my prisoners. "Oh, yes!" said their leader, "we have heard that you did not regard the life of a personal enemy as of any value, but we have seen several men whom you had released who told us that you was quite a different man from the fabulous blood-thirsty Hildebrand we have heard so much about in timid circles."

Upon producing papers which satisfied us that they were neither McNeal's or Leeper's men, but belonged to the command of Col. Beverage of Cape Girardeau, we released them unarmed and afoot. We went on toward Bollinger's Mill, but when in that vicinity on the next morning about sunrise, we met two Federals in the road, who instantly wheeled their horses and dashed through the woods at full speed.

Being burdened with the horses and the arms we had taken from our prisoners on the day previous, all of us could not engage in the pursuit. Captain Snap, myself and two men started after them at full speed, and caught them in less than half a mile. They stopped and threw up their hands before we were within two hundred yards of them. I was almost tempted to shoot them for being cowards.

After taking them back to our boys, we went on the top of an adjacent hill and camped for the day. We ascertained from the prisoners that they were new recruits, which was corroborated by some letters from their friends which they happened to have in their pockets.

Knowing that they had not been in the army long enough to have committed many depredations, we decided to release them; but as we were already burdened with horses we took them along with us to assist with our stock until we had passed Mingo Swamp, and then released them. A few days afterwards we arrived safely in Green county, Arkansas.

CHAPTER XXVI.

Started to St. Francois county, Missouri.—Hung Vogus and Zimmer.—Hung George Hart.—Concealed in Bike Run Hills.—Started back.—Hung Mr. Mett's negro, and another one.—Took two deserters back and hung them.

After remaining a few days with my family, I yielded to the solicitation of Captain Bowman to take a trip to St. Francois county, Missouri, for the purpose of capturing a young man by the name of George Hart, who, on a scout with some militia, had killed Captain Bowman's brother in order to get a very fine horse that he rode.

Our company, consisting of nine men, started on the 20th day of June, 1864; we traveled altogether in the night, and on the morning of the 26th we camped for the day on Wolf creek, about six miles from Farmington. During the day one of my men clad himself in citizen's clothes, which we always carried along for such emergencies, and went into Farmington to see the sights and to get a bottle of good old "tangle-foot."

When night came our man had not made his appearance; we immediately arrested a couple of Dutchmen for the purpose of eliciting information from them concerning the military force in town, thinking that probably my man had been taken in by the soldiers as a spy. The men we arrested were Henry Vogus and John Zimmer, who stated that there were no forces in town at that time, and that there had been no soldiers there for nearly a month. They affirmed that they had been there that day, and that if we did not believe them they would go with us to town and prove the matter. At this juncture my man came in and reported a company of soldiers in the town who had been there for some time. It was now evident to our minds that the Dutchmen were aiming to trap us. I will here state that during the whole war the Dutch went further, tried harder and risked more for my capture than any other people. A very short consultation was sufficient to seal the fate of our two prisoners on the present occasion; we hung them and went on our way rejoicing. Passing a short distance east of Farmington, we stopped at the house of Ross Jelkyl, who was at that time Provost Marshal, and took such things as we needed. Some of my men were anxious to kill him, but he had befriended me on one occasion, and I would not permit them to do so.

From there we went to the residence of Charles Hart, where we found his son George, whom we were after. We stationed men at the back door and demanded admittance at the front; the old man in a short time opened the door, and in obedience to our orders struck a light. On demanding George Hart he made his appearance, looking very much condemned. On asking him about the horse he had taken when he murdered young Bowman, he stated that he had traded him off, and that he was out of the country. We then told him that he must go with us, to which he made no objection, but was very anxious to know what we wished to do with him; we told him to wait and see. Before we had taken him far, he became satisfied that he would be killed, and made us some offers for his life, which Captain Bowman silenced in a few words by asking him if he thought he was able to pay for the life of young Bowman whom he had murdered in cold blood. We traveled about eight miles with our prisoner, during which time he made a complete confession.

Daylight began to appear; we were now about a mile from Big River Mills, and not wishing to be encumbered by a prisoner, we took some hickory bark and hung him to a dogwood sapling. One of his feet touched the ground, so we placed it in the fork of a bush, which completed the process of hanging.

The main object of our trip having been accomplished, our next move was to get supplies of summer clothing for our families, which we decided on taking from an old meddlesome Union German in Jefferson county by the name of Lepp, who had a store on a small creek called Swashen. We accordingly proceeded to the place and found the old man in his store; he was close-fisted and not in the habit of crediting, but we succeeded in getting all we wanted *at very low figures*, and after promising him our patronage in the future we started back.

Knowing that our operations about Farmington would create a great excitement, that the forces at Pilot Knob, Farmington, Potosi, Fredericktown and the Iron Mountain with the irrepressible Big River Militia, would all be put on our trail, we decided to travel by night and to get out of the country as soon as possible. But we were overruled by a power higher than our own, and our plans were in some measure thwarted.

On our way to rob Lepp's store, one of my men complained of feeling unwell, and by the time we had rode ten miles on our return he became too sick to sit upon his horse. We retreated to a cave in the Pike Run hills where we could conceal ourselves, our horses and our goods while administering to the wants of our sick comrade. Our situation here was indeed a very critical one, and had it not been for the kindness of a true Southern friend, who supplied us at night with provisions and horse feed, we undoubtedly would have suffered; he risked his own life to save us, and in addition to his other acts of kindness he procured the services of a physician, who checked the disease in a few days.

It is needless to state that during all this time the country was literally flooded with Federal soldiers who hunted for me on their same old plan, of riding along the road, threatening women and children, and killing chickens.

After remaining at the Pike Run hills seven or eight days, our comrade was sufficiently recovered to mount his horse. As he was yet quite weak we thought it best to travel during daylight at the commencement of our trip. We rode slowly through the woods, and avoided the soldiers by keeping out of the public roads, and by shunning all places where *liquor* could be obtained. On reaching the vicinity of my brothers-in-law, on Flat river, we met old Isaac, a negro belonging to

Mr. Metts, carrying a bridle around his shoulder. As we were dressed in Federal uniform he mistook us for Union soldiers, and in answer to our inquiries, made a lengthy report against the Southern men in that neighborhood, clearly implicating the Simms family as well as the Shannons and Sweeneys. He said he would have reported sooner, but that he was afraid they would suspicion him and get Sam Hildebrand to put him out of the way.

The report he made to us, if told to a squad of Federals, was sufficient to have consigned those Southern men to an ignominious death without any further evidence. The charge was this: that in his opinion "if Sam Hildebrand was to call at their houses and ask for something to eat, that they would feed him until he was as plump as a stuffed turkey." Some of my boys wanted to shoot him to prevent him from making that awful revelation to the Federal authorities; but I objected, because the sound of a gun might lead to our discovery. We quietly lashed him to a horse which we were leading, took him among the hills toward Westover's mill and hung him. On searching his pockets for a knife I found a pocket book containing sixty-four dollars. Some of the boys proposed that as they seemed to have money we should take in a few negroes until our pockets were replenished. On the next day we came suddenly across one in the woods; as we were traveling slowly it was necessary that we should get through the country without being reported. Having no spare rope, we hung the negro with hickory bark; but on searching his pockets we found nothing but a cob pipe.

Nothing else worthy of note occurred until we reached the vicinity of Greenville. While camped for the day on a high elevation, we discovered two men coming up the hill toward us. Under the supposition that they were tracking us, we were about to shoot them, but discovered presently that they were not armed. They came leisurely up the hill, walking as if they were very tired, and got within fifteen steps of our camp before they discovered it. Their first impulse was to run, but we ordered them to surrender, and they abandoned all idea of being able to make their escape. They proved to be deserters from the Federal army at Ironton, who were making their way to their homes at New Madrid. One of my men knew them well, and to him they are indebted to this day for their lives. We kept them with us until night and then permitted them to continue their journey.

We were no little amused at the many horrible tales of pillage and blood-shed that they said were reported daily at the Federal camps about my depredations. The strangest part of it was that many of those enormities were committed on the same day and in localities very remote from each other.

When night came the rest of the company proceeded on to Arkansas; but Captain Bowman, Traster and myself concluded to go into Shannon county after a couple of deserters who, in the early part of the war, had belonged to Captain Bolin's command. While with us, however, they were of no service, being too cowardly to fight and too lazy to steal; but since their desertion they were constantly reporting every squad of rebels who visited that section of country, and were in the habit of annoying Southern citizens in that neighborhood.

On reaching the neighborhood where they lived we learned that they had gone to Ironton, and the supposition was that they had gone there for the purpose of joining the Union army. But on the next day they returned; we quietly arrested them, got them out of the country without creating any alarm and marched them back to Green county, Arkansas, where we hung them in the presence of the command.

CHAPTER XXVII.

Started with nine men to St. Francois county.—Stopped in the Pike
Run Hills.—Robbed the store of Christopher Lepp.—Hung Mr.
Kinder's negro.—Attacked by Federals.—Killed two and lost a
man.—Shot two soldiers on a furlough.—The strange camp.

I had not been at home long before I formed the acquaintance of a man by the
name of Gibson, who had come to our little Green County Confederacy for the
purpose of joining the "bushwhacking department." Gibson was a man possess-
ing some superior advantages over most of Capt. Bolin's men; he had an accomplished education, and was endowed with a peculiar faculty of making all the men
like him. He was the best marksman in our whole company, with one single exception; and that exception, I must modestly assert for the sake of truth, was myself.

On the 16th day of July, I selected Gibson and eight other men for another trip
into St. Francois county. Having made so many failures in that quarter, I had some
forebodings that I would again meet with disappointments; but I had long since
resolved to let my old enemies have no peace while I labored under no greater dis-
advantages than I did. It is true that they were backed by a great nation of untold
wealth, whose enemies actually in the field numbered more than one million and
a half of armed men, and whose line of garrisoned territory extended one hundred and fifty miles south of their nest on Big river; yet while I thought that I was
backed by the South with her armies of three hundred thousand men, I asked no
better amusement than that of striking at my enemies under the ponderous wing
of Federal protection.

Unlike my enemies, I had no commissary department, no steam presses running night and day striking off greenbacks, no outlet to other nations by commercial treaties, no people at my back willing to be saddled with a debt of three or four
thousand millions of dollars merely to carry into effect a Utopian idea. My long
marches had to be made in the night and with the utmost caution and secrecy.
The woods were my home, the moon my orb of light, and the hooting owls my
spectators.

My enemies long since had learned to fear my name; the fear of retributive
justice was sufficient to make them cower; their militia organization only assumed
a tangible shape when I was absent; for on my approach they secreted themselves
so securely that nothing short of the prolonged sound of Gabriel's trump could
ever be able to bring them forth.

We passed quietly through Butler county, along the western line of Madison, then through St. Francois and across Big river to those native hills and hunting grounds of my boyhood, known as the Pike Run hills.

The reader must bear in mind that these hills possess peculiar advantages over any other part of the country between St. Louis and the Arkansas line.

They look like the fragments of a broken up world piled together in dread confusion, and terminating finally in an abrupt bluff on the margin of Big river, where nature has left a cavern half way up the perpendicular rock, now known as "The Hildebrand Cave," the mouth to which cannot be seen either from the top or bottom.

Among these rugged hills, covered over by the dense forest and wild grape vines, are many yawning caverns known to some hunters, while there are doubtless many others never yet seen by the eye of man. We took up our abode in one of these caverns during the inclemency of the weather, and as the ground was too soft to venture out on horseback, for fear of leaving a trail, I went around through the Big river neighborhood on foot, for the purpose of finding some of my enemies. The only one I saw was James Craig; I discovered him one day in the act of leaving home on foot, so I made a circuit through the woods and stationed myself in advance with the intention of arresting him. I wished to take him to my cavern that my comrades also might see him hung; but he never came along, and thus I missed my game entirely.

By this time my men were tired of inaction, so we started on our march, and on going about fifteen miles we came to a place called the Tunnel, on the Iron Mountain railroad.

From the store of Christopher Lepp, we supplied ourselves with all the articles that we could conveniently carry, took our back track to the crossing of Big river, near the ruins of the Hildebrand homestead, and made our way toward Castor creek, for the purpose of squelching a negro belonging to Mr. Kinder. This negro had become notorious for his meddlesome nature, and his propensity for reporting white men. On the night of our arrival there, we succeeded in finding him, and to satisfy ourselves thoroughly in regard to his meanness, we passed ourselves off for Federals, and questioned him concerning his old master. He very freely and exultingly proceeded to relate the many reasons he had for believing that he was disloyal. We asked him whether or not he was willing for us to kill the old man. He told us that he would kill him himself if we would see him out in it; that the soldiers had told him two or three months ago that if he would kill him that he should have the farm, but that as yet he had not succeeded in getting a good opportunity. At this we were satisfied that he would make good food for the buzzards, so we hung him up for that purpose, and started on our way.

We were now traveling in day time and pursuing our way very leisurely, when about four o'clock in the evening, we were trailed up and ran into by a company of Federals, who had probably been trailing us all day. They ran on to us in good earnest, and seemed very anxious for the honor of capturing or killing me. The manner of their attack is worthy of note. On getting within sight of us they held back until we were passing over the backbone of a ridge, then they made a rush, and on getting to the top of the hill were within one hundred yards of us. Their elevation caused them to over shoot all of us except one poor fellow, one of our new recruits, who was shot through the head. We dashed into the brush and went over that rough country about a mile at full speed; then giving up our horses to the other men with directions where to meet us, Gibson, myself and two others, started back on foot to "bushwhack" them. On getting within two hundred yards of where our dead man lay, we saw them exulting over their victory. I directed my men to make their way around and take their positions along the road where they could get a shot, while I took it upon myself to run them back. I crawled up within one hundred yards of the party, got a bead on one of them, and when I fired he fell from his horse within a few feet of where our dead man lay. This was all that was necessary to put them on their back track, and they were off at full speed; as they passed my men they all fired in turn, Gibson brought one to the ground, but I think the other boys missed their aim, although they insisted to the last that they wounded a man apiece.

We secured the horses belonging to the two men we killed, and started on our journey, and on the following morning took up quarters within eight miles of Bloomfield.

During the day, myself and Bill Rucker, walked down to a plum thicket near the road, and while we were there eating plums, we discovered two Dutchmen dressed in citizens' clothes passing by. We called to them to come and get some plums, which they readily consented to do. As we were dressed in Federal uniform they seemed at once to take us for Union soldiers. We asked them to what command they belonged; who they were, and why they were not in the service. They said they belonged to Leeper's command, and were on a furlough to see their uncle living at Mine La Motte, that they had on borrowed clothes and no arms in order to fool the Rebels, should they meet any. We found out a great deal about "Bolin's and Hildebrand's band of murderers and ropers," as they called us. We shot them both, and returned to camp. At night we started on, and in a few days arrived safely at our usual place of crossing the St. Francis.

We arrived on the bank of the river just after dark, and were startled by the appearance of a camp on the other side at the mouth of a little creek. We could easily perceive the reflection from several camp fires among the trees, and more than once we caught the sound of human voices.

Could it be possible that this was a camp of Federals? If so, why did they not place out their pickets? The more we studied about the matter the further were we from coming to any conclusion.

We rode back into the timbered bottom and continued our way down the country at some distance from the river, until we were about a mile below the strange looking camp, and there crossed the river by swimming it.

After continuing up the river a short distance we rode on to a high brushy point and dismounted. Then taking it on foot I proceeded to spy out the mysterious camp above us. I continued to approach cautiously watching closely for the pickets, but I saw nothing of them. Finally I stood in the midst of perhaps a dozen little brush shanties, and yet saw not a single human being. I was more puzzled than ever. I peeped into one of the brush arbors and a lady's voice cried out: "Who is that?" The alarm spread, and I heard the voices of women in every direction.

Presently I heard the voice of my wife, and on going to her I soon learned the particulars of the calamity that had befallen our community in our absence.

CHAPTER XXVIII.

Capt. John, with a company of Federals, burns the Headquarters in Green county, Arkansas.—He is "bushwhacked," routed and killed.—Raid into Washington county with fourteen men.—Attacked by twenty Federals.—Killed a Union man for piloting Capt. John.

A few days before my arrival in Arkansas, our little community of women and children at headquarters, were suddenly aroused from their slumbers one morning by the firing of a gun, and found themselves surrounded by a whole company of Federals under the command of Capt. John from Ironton, Missouri.

All the men were absent on different scouting expeditions, except eight men, who happened to be in camp that morning; they seized their guns and endeavored to make their escape, but seven of them were shot down, and the other made his escape unhurt. The Federals immediately commenced burning the houses, after taking all the provisions and clothing they could find.

The women in great consternation, gathered their children, and in their night clothes huddled together in the centre of the square; there in their helpless condition to watch the devouring flames that was fast winding around them and reducing their homes to ashes.

Before the houses were all in flames however, Capt. John ordered his men to supply the women with what clothing they could snatch from the flames.

After their hasty toilet was concluded their terror subsided, and with perfect composure they watched the progress of the flames without betraying any emotion; they were determined that the Federals should be deprived the satisfaction of believing that they had triumphed over their spirit of eternal enmity to the Federal cause.

Some of our boys who had been out on a hunt now returned toward the camp, and before they were aware the Federals fired upon them and killed two of their number. As the scouts were in the habit of coming in from various directions, it was impossible to give them warning before they were completely in the Federal trap.

A few hours after the tragedy commenced, the Federals had all left, and the women in squads of five or six, went in different directions and camped a few miles off to meet the scouts as they returned.

My wife and her party had camped near the St. Francis river, and were living on fish when I returned. The Federals were still in the neighborhood, burning the farm houses, mills and shops.

On the same night that I learned these particulars, I sent all my men out in different directions to ferret out the enemy and to meet at a designated place before daylight. With much difficulty we succeeded in finding several squads of the Federals, from which we inferred, that finding our men mostly absent, they had divided into many little bands to finish their work of devastating the country as soon as possible.

We met at the time and place designated, and concluded that our only chance was to "bushwhack" the Federals, and thus drive them out of the country as soon as possible. Two men were detailed to take a trip up Black river, to notify Capt. Bolin, and as many men as they could find, of what was going on, that they might intercept the Federals and "bushwhack" them after I should succeed in routing them from the country.

In less than an hour our company was increased to fifteen men. We hastened on foot toward the lower end of the settlement, and on getting within half a mile of a farm house, we saw about thirty Federals engaged in burning the buildings. We heard the discharge of a gun, and on looking in that direction, we saw a Federal reel in his saddle and then fall to the earth. Two soldiers on horseback immediately dashed toward the point where the shot proceeded from, and in an instant we saw a boy about thirteen years of age, crawl out of a gully and start toward the point of the hill where we were with the soldiers after him.

The boy had so much the start of them that we saw he could easily reach us before the Federals could overtake him. We lay concealed in the thick brush and let the boy pass without seeing us; the soldiers were soon in our midst; we rose up and made them surrender without creating any alarm. We tied them securely and awaited the approach of others who might be sent out in search of these two.

The boy was greatly overjoyed when he found out who we were. In about half an hour ten Federals came riding up toward us. Our prisoners had been removed back half a mile and hung to prevent an alarm. We saluted the Federals with a sudden discharge from our rifles, and six of them dropped from their horses; the others suddenly wheeled and made their escape. The other soldiers hastened on to an adjoining ridge and kept up a harmless fire against us for two or three hours; they did this to divert our attention as it appears, for before we were fully aware of the fact a fresh force of Federals, numbering perhaps forty men, commenced a deadly fire upon us in our rear, and soon drove us from our position. Our retreat was rather disorderly, and before we had succeeded in crossing a ravine and gaining the opposite ridge, four of my men were killed and two others slightly wounded. We continued our retreat for five miles, and then placed ourselves in position to rake the Federals without much danger to ourselves. Here we remained for several hours, and were loth to leave the place, but it finally became apparent to us that the intention of the Federals was to burn out the neighborhood, and then to hasten back before we could collect our men together.

We wound our way through the woods toward our old headquarters. Late in the evening we heard firing in front, and in an instant we started in that direction, but were soon met by eight of our men who had just returned from a scout, without knowing what was going on. As they were on the retreat we did not feel justifiable in trying to make a stand against such superior numbers, so we diverged to the right and let the Federals pass without attracting their attention.

On the night following we succeeded in finding the Federal camp, and during the whole night continued to "bushwhack" them at intervals, until we had killed eight or ten of their pickets. The next morning they seemed to have taken up their march for Missouri, but during the whole day we annoyed them all we could, by posting ourselves in positions where we had the advantage, and thereby picked off several of them. Late in the evening they made an attempt to follow us into the woods, but we attacked the party on every side; the slaughter was terrible, and we finally put them to rout after killing Capt. John himself, and quite a number of his men.

We discovered among the Federals, several citizens, whom we afterwards learned had gone from Missouri for the purpose of giving all the assistance in their power toward ferreting out our headquarters.

Wearied by constant fighting, I and my men now returned to the neighborhood of our old camp, leaving a fresh supply of Capt. Bolin's men to continue "bushwhacking" the Federals until they should return to their hive in Ironton.

After we had completely routed Capt. John's incendiaries and driven them from the country, our condition was indeed deplorable.

Without shelter for our families save a few huts that the Federals did not consider worth burning, into each of which two or three families were huddled, without bedding or a change of clothing, and but little food, we were indeed in adverse circumstances. Several of our men were compelled to remain at headquarters several months to repair damages. Our families, in their crowded condition, became unhealthy, and several of the children died. While we were arranging matters for the comfort and convenience of our families, we obtained our supplies from the border counties of Missouri by making short raids; our bedding and provisions, however, we obtained in a great measure, from our friends; but we occasionally branched out further to rob the stores and houses of Union men.

Another great difficulty under which we labored was the entire absence of surgical aid for our wounded, for the want of which many of our men who recovered were so deformed that they were forever afterward rendered unfit for active duty.

The whole available force of our community now only amounted to eighty available men, and by the time that we had rebuilt twenty houses and a temporary mill, our numbers were still further reduced by desertion, for many of them now left and went into Texas. While these repairs were going on we held a council, in which it was decided that half our men might take the field against our enemies in Missouri, and make them pay for the damage that we had sustained. In doing this, however, we had no intention of applying the torch to the dwellings of our Union enemies; we were never mean enough for that; we made no war upon women and children; that kind of warfare was exclusively used by our enemies of boasted civilization, refinement and magnanimity.

I started to Washington county, Missouri, with fourteen men to obtain supplies of clothing and ammunition. With a great deal of caution we made our way up Black river through Butler and Reynolds counties, and entered Washington county on her extreme southern line, traveling only at night, and concealing ourselves each day among the rugged hills of Black river.

We visited a store and packed several horses which we had taken in the neighborhood, with shoes, domestics and calicoes; and here we found some concealed ammunition, which we appropriated. On starting back we traveled slowly; not having heard of any Federals in the neighborhood, we imagined ourselves safe, and designed traveling in the day time. As we were so familiar with all the roads and by-paths in this section of country, we generally felt safe while on our return to Arkansas, but on this occasion we were doomed to disappointment.

We had gone but a short distance into Reynolds county, when we were suddenly attacked by a party of Federals, numbering perhaps twenty or twenty-five; they had trailed us from the store we had robbed, and now they came upon us with a perfect fury.

Being heavily packed and encumbered with the horses we were leading, we could not run; at their fire one of my men was killed, at which I took advantage of their empty guns, wheeled my men into the brush, dismounted, and in an instant returned their fire, at which three of their number fell; I dashed forward with about half my men and succeeded in gaining their rear. My party in front and my men in the rear now made a simultaneous charge upon them with our revolvers, killing two more and wounding several, in which two of my men were wounded, but not mortally.

In the fight all the other Federals charged over us and got away, with the exception of eight prisoners, three of whom were wounded. The result of the little fight was, five dead Federals, thirteen horses, eighteen guns and ten revolvers; having lost one man killed and two wounded, but not sufficiently to keep them from traveling.

After I had inspected the damages, I turned my attention to the prisoners, who were dismounted, disarmed and sitting by the roadside, under guard. On approaching them two of them arose, called me by name and asked permission to shake hands with me. After a short conversation I found that they were two of the men I had captured on Lost creek, in Wayne county, during the month of May, 1863, whom I released after negotiating with them for the escape of two of Capt. Bolin's men in prison at Ironton. On recognizing them I again gave them my hand in reassurance that I appreciated the services they had rendered us in proving true to their word, and could not help telling them that I was glad to see them. After the ceremony incident to the renewal of our acquaintance was over, I began making preparations for continuing our journey after having first buried the dead.

I told our two Union friends that they were again released, together with their three wounded comrades, but that I would take the other three along with me;

they, however, plead manfully for the release of their three friends, but I told them that I was compelled to have their assistance in getting along with our stock, until we reached Greenville, at which place, for their sake, I would release them, and true to my word, I did so.

We made our way to Green county with as much haste as prudence would permit; being too much burdened to "bushwhack" any of those citizens who had accompanied Capt. John into our little confederacy, we concluded to let them rest for the present; but having accidentally met one in the road, I shot him through the head and rode on. We found all things cheerful about headquarters, and soon divided our goods among the needy families.

CHAPTER XXIX.

Took a raid into Missouri with four men.—Killed a Federal.—Killed two of Capt. Milks' men.—Started to De Soto.—Routed by the Federals.—Adventure with a German.—Killed three Federals on Black river.

In the latter part of August, 1864, I selected four men and started after some of my old enemies on Big river.

At this period they had all disappeared except three or four who still ventured to call their old residences their homes, but they stayed most of their time around the Federal camps anxiously waiting for the time to come when the Federal authorities would succeed, either in killing or capturing me, when a new era of peace and quiet would again bless them in the pursuit of theft and murder.

Those of the old mob who had left their homes and were now dwelling, as they supposed, in utter obscurity, were not lost sight of by me, for I kept myself posted in regard to all their movements. The especial object of this trip was to penetrate the enemies country as far as De Soto, Jefferson county, Missouri, and surprise a couple of the old mob who now lived in that vicinity, and before the authorities were aware of our unholy presence, to have our little mission of vengeance completed. On passing Bloomfield it might truthfully be said that we were within the Federal lines. A heavy military force was stationed at Pilot Knob at the beginning of the war, and smaller forces were stationed at the county seats of the various counties in Southeast Missouri; they were inactive so far as the national war was concerned, but amused themselves by marauding through the country, and occasionally killing some unarmed citizens, or indulging in the characteristics of Ben. Butler.

On gaining the vicinity of Fredericktown, we obtained important information from our friends in that quarter relative to the distribution of the Federal forces, which aided us materially in shaping our course. From this place we went east of Mine La Motte, and took up our quarters for the day in an unfrequented part of the country, about three miles south of the Cross Roads, in St. Francois county, where we remained unmolested until in the evening, when we discovered a man in Federal uniform tracking our horses slowly across an adjoining ridge. We felt very sorry for him in his lonely condition; I went down the hill a little distance toward him, and when he came within a hundred yards of me, and commenced making his circuit toward our camp I turned old "Kill-devil" loose upon him; but owing to his stooping posture as he was looking for tracks I shot him too low and broke him down in the back. He set up a hideous yelling, which was very annoying to us just at this time; so I hastened to his relief, and soon dispatched him with my revolver. Being a little fearful that we had attracted the attention of the people in the neighborhood, and that perhaps a Union force was on our track of which the lone Federal might have been one of the number, we concluded to move. Directing our way through the most thickly wooded parts of the country during the balance of the day, we reached Wolf creek about midnight at the plank road leading from Farmington to Ste. Genevieve.

Feeling much fatigued, and having lost much sleep, we decided on camping until the following night, having with us a sufficiency of provisions and horse feed. We slept soundly until daylight, and then did picket duty by turns until late in the evening, when I discovered two Federal soldiers in the valley below us, going toward Farmington. I at once took my position with one of my men, and as they came up talking very merrily, we surprised them by presenting our pistols in a few feet of their faces and demanding a surrender, at which they seemed somewhat alarmed but made no resistance.

After dismounting and disarming them we took them to our quiet nook in the woods, and upon inquiry we found that they belonged to a company at Ste. Genevieve under Capt. Milks.

We felt very much rejoiced at getting two of this company who had formerly been stationed at Farmington, and after harrassing and robbing the peaceable citizens in that community for several months they were removed to Ste. Genevieve.

On one of their scouts through the country they arrested Charles Burks, county judge of Ste. Genevieve for compelling the Provost Marshal to deliver up some horses belonging to the judge whom the marshal had unjustly seized. The old man was taken a few miles after his arrest by Milks' men and shot without any questions being asked, and without even a charge of disloyalty ever having been brought against him. On another occasion they arrested Irvin M. Haile, one of the most peaceable men in St. Francois county, under a charge made by some sneaking informer, that on one occasion he had fed me and my men. This was the whole of the accusation brought against him. He was allowed no trial, no defense; but two inhuman monsters took him a few miles, shot him through the head, then taking his horse they left his body in the woods, where it was afterwards found.

The recollection of these and some other acts of atrocity committed by that company sealed the fate of my two prisoners; in the name of justice and humanity I shot them both through the head with my revolver, and ordered my men to cast them in a deep hole of water in Wolf creek, with stones tied to their feet.

As soon as it was dark we went to the house of a friend to get some feed for ourselves and horses, but on arriving there we saw a party of perhaps twenty persons who were just mounting their horses in front of the gate, and in a few minutes they rode off and were lost to us in the dim starlight. We approached the house cautiously, but found no one there except the kind lady who told us that the cause of the excitement was that "Sam Hildebrand was supposed to be in country;" that some soldiers from Fredericktown had come up and stated positively that my trail had been followed in that direction, and that the citizens were ordered out to assist in the search.

After getting something to eat and feed for our horses we started on, and by daylight the next morning we were safely housed in a cave among the Pike Run hills, in the northern part of St. Francois county.

Here we remained but one day; as soon as darkness approached we proceeded on into Jefferson county until ten o'clock, when we stopped at the house of a friend who gave us our suppers and treated us so well that the night was half spent before we started on. Our friend warned us very pressingly against going any further in the direction of De Soto, but we determined not to retreat until real danger was apparent. But unfortunately we had consumed too much time, and did not reach the part of the country where we designed taking up quarters for the day, and while making a forced march between daylight and sunrise on an old unfrequented road near the top of a ridge where we designed taking up quarters, we suddenly ran into a company of Federal soldiers who were coming toward us.

They charged us on sight and in good earnest, firing a volley at us, but we miraculously escaped unhurt, but several of us carried off some respectable holes in our clothing. Their charge was really furious, and caused us to scatter in every direction, and after a hasty and precipitate retreat of perhaps a mile and a half, I ventured to stop and take a look at my surroundings; the last fifteen minutes of my life passed off in such a "whiz" that I hardly knew where I was, and I was very certain that I did not know where my men were; but I felt very well over the fact that there were no Federal soldiers in sight.

I was not long in planning my course; a place had been designated by me in the Pike Run hills for us to meet in an emergency of this kind, and I struck out for the spot, traveling very cautiously and keeping in the thickest timbered country all the time.

Arriving at the place late in the evening, I found one of my men who had gained the spot a short time before me. Here we remained waiting in anxious suspense until after dark, and had almost come to the conclusion that the other men had been captured or killed when they came up. They had got together soon after the stampede, and not being very well acquainted with the country they had been lost, and when night overtook them they pressed a pilot into their service whom they discovered passing along the road, and compelled him to accompany them to the place. The pilot I knew very well, and after deceiving him in regard to the course we designed taking, we released him under the promise that he would not report us.

As we were now destined to be hunted down like the wild beasts of the forest, we resolved to get out of the country as quick as possible and over some country not traveled by us heretofore. We started in a westwardly direction, and after traveling a few miles stopped at the house of a friend for our suppers.

Crossing the Iron Mountain railroad south of Blackwell's Station, we gained the vicinity of the Old Mines, in Washington county, before it was yet light, where we took up quarters for the day. One of my men being acquainted in the neighborhood, we had no trouble in getting our necessary provisions and horse feed.

While we made our brief sojourn in this locality an incident worth relating occurred, which was very amusing to us, and may not be uninteresting to the reader. About ten o'clock in the forenoon, while it was my turn to stand on picket I sauntered through the thick brush down to the main road, distant about two hundred yards, and suddenly ran on to a German who was sitting near the road side, sheltered from the sun by some brush. I discovered him before he saw me. He held in his hand an old double-barreled shot gun. As he had on an old suit of Federal uniform, my first impulse was to draw my revolver, which I did in an instant. As soon as the German saw me he sprang to his feet, let his old gun fall to the ground and threw up his hands. Seeing that I was dressed in Federal uniform, he immediately cried out that he was "all right," and began in a hurried, broken gibberish to give an account of himself; that he was from De Soto, and was going to a saw mill west of Potosi; that he was a discharged Union soldier; that Sam Hildebrand was in the country about De Soto, and that he was afraid to stay there on that account. At this I advanced toward him and extended my hand, saying as I did so that I was really a little frightened, that I thought he was Sam Hildebrand himself when I first saw him; that I would not hurt him if he was a Union man, but that I came very near shooting him under the mistaken idea that he was Hildebrand. He laughed heartily at the coincident and was quite merry over the happy turn that the affair had taken.

I told him that I had some men stationed back in the woods on one of Hildebrand's old trails, and that he could go with me and form one of my party for the day, to which he gladly consented, manifesting a great deal of gratitude. As we made our way cautiously to the camp through the thick brush I told him that he was running a great risk in traveling through that portion of country, for it was one of Hildebrand's main passways.

On coming up to the boys in camp he did not wait for an introduction, but stepped in ahead of me and shook hands with them all in the greatest glee, telling as he did so a great many things he knew about "Sam Hildebrand."

The boys seemed to understand the matter perfectly well without any explanations from me, and humored the joke very well by asking the most absurd questions about my barbarity; but none of the questions were too hard, for he answered them all, making it appear that I was a blood-thirsty barbarian, without an equal in the world's history.

It was not until sometime during the afternoon that we undeceived him in regard to the true nature of things; it was sometime before he could comprehend the sudden change, or be made to believe that he was really in my hands. But as he gradually became convinced of the fact he began a series of lies that would have shamed "Baron Munchausen" himself. We stopped him short, however, and told him that if he would not report us for one month we would let him go, at which he sprang at me, seizing my hand with both of his, he pledged himself and swore by all that was holy and righteous that he never would report us while he lived. He shook hands with us all and started, looking back every ten feet until he was out of sight, then he seemed to double his speed until he was out of hearing.

While the sun was yet an hour high we started on our way, keeping in the woods until dark, then passing west of Potosi, by traveling all night, we reached a point near the town of Centreville, in Reynolds county, where we obtained feed for ourselves and horses.

In traveling down Black river late one evening we ran into a squad of Federals, six in number, whom we charged in a furious manner, firing on them with our revolvers. They did not return our fire, but ran most gloriously. We killed one and captured two more; those we captured stated that they belonged to Leeper's command; this being the case of course we shot them.

We took their horses and arms, made another night's journey, and arrived safely in Green county, Arkansas. There I found a dispatch for me from Gen. Sterling Price, requesting me to take charge of the advance guard of his army, as he was "going up to possess Missouri," to which I most gladly consented on conditions that I would be released as soon as we should reach the vicinity of my old home on Big river.

CHAPTER XXX.

Commanded the advance guard in Price's raid.—The Federals burn
   Doniphan.—Routed them completely.—Captured some at Patterson.—Killed Abright at Farmington.—Left Price's army.—Killed
   four Federals.—Maj. Montgomery storms Big River Mills.—Narrow escape from capture.

It is not my purpose to give a history of Price's raid into Missouri further than
to narrate a few facts connected with my own operations.

In September, 1864, by request, I took charge of the advance guard after all
arrangements were made for the grand campaign. The dispatch that came to me,
having stated that General Price designed taking Missouri and holding it, I felt
that a great honor was conferred upon me, and was pleased beyond measure
with the prospect of being once more enabled to triumph over my enemies and to
peaceably establish myself at the home of my childhood, among the blissful scenes
of my earlier years.

While these day-dreams were passing through my excited imagination, I repaired to the designated point and found that my command consisted of a party of
ragged Missourians, about forty in number, some of whom I knew. Keeping pace
with the main body of the army, we traveled not more than fifteen miles each day.
Nothing of importance occurred until we reached the town of Doniphan in Ripley
county, Missouri; when, on approaching the place, we discovered large volumes
of smoke arising from the town. We put spurs to our horses and hastened into the
place as soon as possible; finding that the Federals in evacuating the place, had set
fire to every house but one, and that belonged to a Federal officer, we concluded
that it had better burn also. We arrived in time to save the mill which seemed to
have burned very slowly. It appears that McNeal's and Leeper's men were on their
way to burn up our Green County Confederacy, but ascertaining that Price was on
his march for Missouri they set fire to the town and decamped. We pursued and
overtook them before they got to Greenville, had a little skirmish, lost two men
killed and four wounded, captured sixteen Federals and shot them, rushed on to
the town of Patterson, captured eleven negroes and seven white men in Federal
uniform and shot them. While the main army advanced slowly I scouted in front
of it with my command; but Federals and Union men were very scarce; I still held
the advance however, passing through Greenville, Bloomfield, Fredericktown and
Farmington; all of which were evacuated before our arrival, and through which I
passed with my force without molesting anyone with one exception. On reaching
Farmington no resistance was offered; the people were somewhat alarmed, but

all surrendered quietly except a German, named Abright, who ran when we approached, refused to halt, and was shot of course.

Finally, reaching the Iron Mountain Railroad at Mineral Point, we tore up the road, burned several bridges, and tore down the telegraph; but finding no one to kill, I left the command, according to previous agreement, and hastened to the neighborhood of my personal enemies. Finding none of them there to kill I employed myself in recruiting for the Southern army, and succeeded in the short space of six days in getting a full company, who were sworn in, and under Capt. Holmes went into the Southern service. While laboring for the cause of the South I was at the residence of Maj. Dick Berryman at the stone house in Bogy's Lead Mines, near Big river, with a portion of Capt. Holmes' men, when four Federals who had escaped from the fort at Ironton during the siege, came along the road; with but little difficulty we effected their capture, shot them and threw their bodies into a mineral hole.

The main army did not remain long in our section of country; Gen. Price indeed was a great military chieftain, but his present campaign through Missouri seemed to lack design; from the time he entered the State until he left it, he garrisoned no posts in the rear. Pilot Knob, the terminus of the railroad from St. Louis and the depot for supplies for all Southeast Missouri was taken, and then abandoned on the next day; he made his way to Missouri river and then up that stream in the direction of Kansas for several hundred miles without molestation leaving St. Louis, the great commercial key of the West, almost "spoiling to be taken." The great Missouri chieftain left St. Louis to his right, while the heavy force at that place were quietly taking possession of the abandoned posts in his rear. If he had joined the "Independent Bushwhacking Department of the Confederate States of America" with all his men, in less than thirty days there would not have been a Federal soldier west of the Mississippi. While Maj. Berryman and a few other officers stayed in St. Francois county recruiting, the main army gained the Missouri river and was quietly making a blind march in the direction of Idaho.

The Federal forces took possession of the Iron Mountain railroad, and on one pleasant afternoon in October, our new recruits armed with their shot guns and squirrel rifles were run into by Maj. Montgomery of the Sixth Missouri Cavalry and completely routed, in which their loss was seven killed and all the balance missing. Montgomery also killed several citizens, whose names were Fite, Vandover, and Judge Haile, the father of Irvine M. Haile, who was previously murdered by Milks' men.

On the day before Maj. Montgomery routed the new recruits at Big River Mills, I went with some men to Cadet on the railroad and took from the store of Mr. Kellerman a wagon load of goods which I delivered up to Maj. Berryman, who distributed them among his men. Maj. Montgomery, with two companies of the Sixth Missouri Cavalry, struck our trail and followed us nearly into camp; but when he ran into the pickets they obeyed the orders I had previously given, and ran in a different direction from the camp, thereby leading the Federals away from our squad of raw recruits, and giving them time to escape. I was not at Big River Mills when Montgomery stormed the place, but was at St. Joseph Lead Mines, when he passed. I was sitting on my horse talking to a lady, when the first thing that I saw of them they were within a few yards of me; I assumed an air of unconcern and continued the conversation; on discovering that they were eyeing me very closely, I turned my horse and rode within a few feet of the column in the direction they were going, talking back to the lady until I was too far off to continue the conversation. I then found myself near a lieutenant whom I addressed as captain, asking him in a very awkward manner if he was going to Big River Mills to drive the Rebels off, which he answered in the affirmative. I told him that I would like to help if I had a gun, but he told me very curtly that he wanted no men who were not drilled. My horse seemed to be a little lame and I gradually fell back, talking all the time to the man opposite me until the last one had passed. I kicked and "cussed" my horse to try to keep up but I could not do it. On getting about one hundred yards behind I availed myself of an opportunity at a turn in the road and took to the woods; the lameness of my horse was very much improved, but I could not beat them into the town; however, I knew that the pickets would lead them off some other way. They did so, but were overtaken and killed at the ford above the mill pond.

The new recruits were within hearing of the guns and "broke for tall timber." The short sojourn of the Confederate forces in Missouri was indeed a severe blow to the course I had marked out for myself. In my excited imagination I had raised the veil and looked down the vista of time, beheld the Southern arms triumphant, our country again restored to peace and prosperity, and my little family and my aged mother leaning upon my arm for support at the old homestead, surrounded by all the endearments of our once happy days. But I was awakened from my dream by the unhappy termination of Price's raid; it impressed my mind very forcibly with the fact that the people of Missouri were tired of the war and would sacrifice but little more at the shrine of their political convictions. In fact a large majority of them were compelled by circumstances beyond their control to remain at home and take their chances. The atrocities committed in their midst by men professing Union sentiments finally failed to elicit from them a casual remark.

When the war began, the American people were untutored in regard to the cruelties of war; in fact, I am inclined to the opinion that there was not a nation upon earth which had formed the most remote conception of the cruelties of the American people, with all their boasted moral and religious training. Even the words of political bias expressed in times of peace, many years before the war commenced, while yet almost the whole nation was of the same opinion, were treasured up and resurrected against certain citizens, for which their lives were taken.

From a contemplation of this unwelcome subject I turned my mind, and through my native woods I traveled alone to my home in Arkansas, with my fond hopes crushed, and my spirits below zero.

CHAPTER XXXI.

Selected three men and went to Missouri to avenge the death of Rev. William Polk.—Got ammunition in Fredericktown.—Killed the German who informed on Polk.—Returned to Arkansas.

After recruiting our horses and making all necessary arrangements for the comfort and convenience of my family in my absence, I selected three men and started to Madison county, Missouri, for the express purpose of killing the German who reported on preacher Polk, and by whose instigation his murder, by the Union soldiers, had been brought about.

That venerable Baptist minister, William Polk, was about seventy years of age, and had been preaching for about forty years. As a christian of unquestionable piety no man ever stood higher; as a citizen his conduct was irreproachable, and as to his loyalty and patriotism it never before was brought into question. From his lips no word had ever dropped that could be construed into an expression of sympathy for the Southern rebellion.

In the latter part of October, 1864, three Federal soldiers rode up to his house to rob him first and then kill him.

They demanded his money which he gave up, amounting to twenty dollars, he told them that he had no more, at which they replied that twenty dollars was not enough to save his life.

They took him out of the yard, when a Federal soldier by the name of Robert Manning shot him through the head.

Believing that the German informer was the most guilty one in this transaction, I was willing to attempt his capture even at this inclement season of the year.

Camping out in the woods was disagreeable; stopping at the houses of our friends at night was extremely dangerous; and if a snow should happen to fall, thereby exposing our trail to the Federals we would be under the necessity of running a horse race for nearly two hundred miles.

On reaching the St. Francis we found it considerably swollen from recent rains higher up the river. I proceeded at once to swim it, and arrived safely at the opposite bank, but my three men having entered the river too near together their horses crowded each other, which caused them to beat down with the current until one of my men named Swan washed into a drift and came near being drowned before I could pull off my coat and boots and swim to his rescue. I got to him in time to pull him out on to a drift, but his horse washed under it and we saw him no more.

After we had all got over we built a fire, dried our clothes and camped for the night.

Swan did not feel well the next morning, so he concluded to make an effort to get back to headquarters, while we proceeded on with our journey, traveling only twenty or twenty-five miles per day, stopping with our friends on the way.

On reaching Madison county we began to look out for Federal squads, as there were two or three hundred troops quartered in Fredericktown. My ammunition was getting very scarce and I felt as though I would be compelled to stop and see my old friends in town. We secreted ourselves and horses about a mile from the place, and as daylight was near at hand we had to lay over for the day; on the following night I made my way cautiously, and crawled into an alley near the residence of my friend, when a dog espied me and tried to make me retreat; I tried to negotiate with him, offering him as I thought everything that was fair, but all to no purpose. About ten o'clock, all things being favorable, I went around to the opposite side of town and started in through an open street, walking leisurely, but keeping near the buildings. When I had got fairly into town I came suddenly on a Federal picket at the corner of a block, who accosted me by inquiring: "Where are you going, Bill?" I answered in a whisper "after some whisky;" "all right" said he, "bring a fellow a snort." By this time I was out of whispering distance, and soon came to a large saloon on the corner, passed around to the other side which was closed up, and amused myself several minutes in looking in at the window. I saw quite a number of the Federals, some playing cards, some amusing themselves in various ways, and all of them seemed to be enjoying themselves very well. I made my way to the house of my friend, climbed over the plank fence, and gave a peculiar wrap at the back door which was well understood. I got a lunch, some good brandy, plenty of ammunition, rations to last two days, and some very important information. I went out through the alleys as a matter of choice, the smaller dogs being posted in the alleys and the larger ones in the streets. As the night was half spent we went into the neighborhood of Mr. O'Banyon and camped in the woods until the next evening, when we made our way over to the German's who was accused of laying the plot for the murder of Elder Polk.

Dressed in Federal uniform, we rode up to his house as the sun was going down, were taken for Federal soldiers and received with a great deal of cordiality. We had talked to him but a short time when the subject of "Preacher Polk" was introduced. The German in a boastful manner gave us the history of his transactions in the matter, fully confirming his complicity in the murder. We marched him off into the woods near the farm of Mr. North, where I talked all the Dutch language to him that I knew, and after giving him distinctly to understand that "hog killing time" had come, I shot him.

As soon as it was dark we rode back to the suburbs of Fredericktown for the purpose of silencing a Union citizen of that place who had made himself rather officious in reporting citizens for disloyalty, and for accusing certain ones of having fed "Sam Hildebrand."

I left one of my men with the horses, and taking the other, I went into town and knocked at the door, our call was answered by a lady who innocently told us that the man for whom we inquired had gone to St. Louis, at which we politely bid her good night and left the town. We hurried on to Castor creek to the house of a friend whose hospitalities we enjoyed for several days, while we were endeavoring by every means in our power to take in a certain man who lived in that neighborhood; but the excitement we had raised by squelching the German rendered our intended victim very shy. Finally we went to his house just after dark one night and called for him, but his wife declared that he was not at home. We made a diligent search through every room, but not finding him we started for Cape Girardeau county for the purpose of obtaining some supplies for the winter. We succeeded in getting all that we could conveniently pack, and started for Arkansas. We saw but one squad of Federals on our homeward trip; we were passing through Stoddard county, east of Bloomfield, when a party of about ten came up behind us, but they fired upon us before they got near enough to do any harm, and by taking to the woods we made our escape. They might easily have compelled us to throw away our goods to facilitate our flight, if they had felt disposed to continue the pursuit. As it was they never got in sight of us any more, and although our horses were much jaded we made very good time until dark and then proceeded on more slowly. We swam the St. Francis without much trouble and landed home safely.

I found my wife and children well, but Mr. Swan, whom I had rescued from the turbid waters of the St. Francis had sickened and died during our absence, and had been buried a few hours before our arrival.

CHAPTER XXXII.

Started with eight men on a trip to Arkansas river.—Hung a "Scallawag" on White river—Went into Conway county.—Treachery of a negro on Point Remove.—"Foot burning" atrocities.—Started back and hung a renegade.

During the early part of the winter of 1864, several persons from the vicinity of Lewisburg, Arkansas, came to our Headquarters and reported trouble with the negroes and scallawags in that part of the State.

Lewisburg is a small town on the north side of the Arkansas river, about fifty miles above Little Rock; the country around this place is very fertile, and before the war, was inhabited by a wealthy class of farmers of the highest cast of honor and intelligence, the most of whom owned a large number of slaves. It seems that as soon as the ordinance emancipating the slaves was enforced in that part of the country, several scallawags from the free States, slipped in among the negroes, whose especial duty seemed to be to incite the negroes to deeds of villainy.

About Lewisburg they seemed to have been very successful in their mission as insurrectionists, and the continued reports from that quarter convinced us that a short campaign among them during the winter might be beneficial. In January, 1865, I started with eight men, we passed through Lawrence and Independence counties, and on reaching the beautiful country bordering on White river, which had been in a high state of cultivation before the war, but now sadly neglected, we approached near the town of Batesville, when we learned that two or three of the very animals we were hunting for were in that "neck of the woods." I left six of my men with our horses in a dense thicket, and three of us started out separately to visit the negro cabins.

I had not proceeded far before I entered a dirty cabin of "colored people," whom I greeted very warmly. The household consisted of an old man and woman, each about sixty years of age, and about six others who were grown. The old man treated me with great politeness, and would persist in calling me "Massa," notwithstanding my repeated objections. I talked to them some time on the subject of their freedom; the old man gave me distinctly to understand that he considered their condition much worsted by the change; but the youngsters seemed to be in a high glee over their future prospects. I succeeded in gaining their confidence by professing intense loyalty to their cause, and ascertained beyond all doubt that a "Bosting man" had been through the neighborhood to obtain their names and their pledges to support him for Congress as soon as the war should close, with the solemn promise from him that he would have all the land and the property of the whites confiscated and given to them.

One of the boys showed me a paper which he said was a certificate that he was to be the owner of the Anthony House in Little Rock. On inquiring where I could find my "Bosting brother," they told me that he was "down about Lewisburg raising money from the Rebels to build school houses for the colored people."

After intimating that I was an officer of the Freedman's Bureau, I was about to depart, when a tall, lank specimen of a genuine Eastern philanthropist made his appearance at the door. After being assured that I was "all right," he remarked that he had been in the neighborhood several days, and had made out a report of all the property which would be confiscated as soon as he returned to Washington. He proceeded to draw it out from the lining of his hat and handed it to me to read, I fumbled about in my pockets for some time, and then remarked that I had lost my spectacles; he then took the paper and read it with a great deal of pomposity, commenting occasionally on the names as he read them off.

I sanctioned the report heartily, and told him that it was bound to win. He then remarked to the negroes that any assistance they could render him in the way of money matters, would be thankfully received, as he was working for their good alone. They contributed all the money they had, which I think amounted to about six dollars. I arose to depart, stating that I had promised to take dinner with some colored friends about a mile from there, and insisted that my "brother missionary" accompany me, to which he readily consented.

During our walk he laid before me many of his plots and plans, which fully convinced me that he designated to excite the minds of the negroes with the hope of ultimately expelling all the white people from the State, except their immediate friends from the North.

We finally arrived at the place, but it proved to be a Rebel camp instead of a negro cabin. On coming up to the boys my missionary seemed to be badly alarmed, but made no show of resistance. We hung the scallawag to a limb, where he remained until we got our dinner, then we took him down and threw him into a hole of water, with a large stone tied to his feet. We crossed White river at a ferry several miles below Batesville, immediately after which we came suddenly upon a company of twenty armed men dressed in citizen's clothes. As we were not posted in regard to the state of affairs in that part of the State, we were utterly at a loss to know to which side they belonged in this war.

We were first seen by a tall, awkward looking specimen of humanity, who stepped out in front of us and questioned us about who we were and where we were going.

He held in his hand a double-barreled gun large enough to have killed all eight of us at one fire. Without answering his questions, as we wished to take items before committing ourselves, I asked "where is your Captain?" He replied that he was going to serve as captain himself, and immediately made a remark that led us to understand that they were merely a party starting out on a "bear hunt."

At night we stopped at the Round Pond, and ascertained that there was but little Union sentiment in that part of the State, and that we would meet with no trouble from the Federals until we got into the counties bordering on Arkansas river. We avoided a military camp at Clinton, not knowing to a certainty whether they were Rebels or not.

We had no source of information upon which we could explicitly rely. On arriving in Conway county we stayed all night with an old gentleman on Point Remove; but being fearful that our horses might be stolen, we concluded to sleep under a shed between the stable and the smokehouse.

About one o'clock in the night we saw two negroes approaching the smoke house very cautiously; after some little time they succeeded in removing a log, when one of them crawled in. We made an attempt to arrest the one on the outside, but he got away, followed by two shots, which, however, missed him. A great consternation was produced in the house, and out the old man came with a light. On taking our prisoner out he made a clean breast of it; he confessed that he belonged to a band of eight negroes, who were camped on the bank of Arkansas river, between Point Remove and Gilmore's Landing; that they were led by a white man, and were in the habit of robbing white people, and making them tell where their money was concealed by burning their feet.

On the next morning he consented to pilot us to the place where they were camped; but instead of taking us directly to the place, he took us a mile around through the cane, and finally brought us back to within two hundred yards of where we had been before, and then pointed to their camp. Here it was, sure enough, but the birds had flown.

For this trick the body of a dead negro was soon discovered floating down the muddy river.

I was much mortified in thus failing to squelch the foot-burning scallawag who was leading the negroes on to such acts of cruelty; but he succeeded in getting away and is no doubt by this time in Congress.

After remaining in the woods a few miles from Lewisburg for several days without being able to do any good toward ferreting out the "foot-burners," we started back through Van Buren and Izard counties without molesting any one until we got near a little town called Mount Olive, where we captured a man whom we accidentally met in the road. Several of my men knew him, and stated that he had been run off from Bloomfield, Missouri, for professing loyalty during the second year of the war, and thus betraying the confidence his neighbors had hitherto placed in him. He was also accused of having had a man shot near Bloomfield, by reporting on him; this accusation he virtually acknowledged after we had captured him.

We took him a few hundred yards from the road, hung him to a limb, and proceeded on through Lawrence county to our old headquarters.

CHAPTER XXXIII.

Gloomy prospects for the South. Takes a trip to Missouri with four men. Saved from capture by a woman. Visits his mother on Big river. Robs the store of J. V. Tyler at Big River Mills.—Escapes to Arkansas.

I had a long conversation with Capt. Bolin, who had just returned from an expedition on the head waters of Current river, concerning the probable termination of the war.

He was a man of considerable intelligence, and I always noticed on his return from a raid his pockets were stuffed full of Yankee newspapers.

I found him sitting on a log deeply absorbed in examining his miscellaneous pile of news.

"Well, Captain! what's the news from the North? Are they ready to give it up yet?"

"Give it up, indeed! Sam, the war is very near to a close."

"I thought so! I knew they could not hold out much longer; I suppose we have killed nearly half of them; I hope they will grin and bear it until we get another swipe at them!"

"I rather think they will! but Sam, it is the South which is going under; her fate is already sealed."

"What makes you think so?"

"I think so because the great armies of the Confederacy are crippled and almost annihilated; their whole country is overrun and impoverished by immense Northern armies; I fear that our great chieftains, will be compelled to yield, and when they go under, our little fighting here must also stop."

"Ah, Captain, you get that from your Yankee papers; I can't believe anything that they contain."

I must acknowledge however, that I was somewhat staggered by Capt. Bolin's candid remarks. I immediately selected four men, being determined to make another trip to see whether the Federals had literally swallowed up the whole country or not.

We made our way up Black river, thinking that we would be very likely to make the trip on that route without ever seeing a Federal.

One evening, on the first day of March, 1865, after remaining in a thicket nearly all day, we concluded to approach the house of a friend with whom we had stopped on a previous trip. A terrible rain storm was coming up, and we thought we could leave our horses where they were and repair to the house for shelter until the rain should cease.

Our friend was from home; he had gone toward Springfield to look after his son whom he feared had been murdered by some of the roving bands of Federals. We learned from the good woman that none of the enemy had passed that road for a long time; so feeling perfectly safe we repaired to the barn intending to get a little sleep, but took the precaution to crawl up into the loft and over the hay into a low place near the wall.

Directly after dark we were awakened by the noise of a large empty wagon that was driven up to the barn, just under our window; on peeping out the truth flashed across our minds in an instant that not less than fifty Federal soldiers were in the barn yard all around us; but on watching their maneuvers a few minutes, we became satisfied that they knew nothing of our presence.

The barn floor below us was soon full of them, and in a few minutes eight or ten of them crawled up through the window on to the hay and rolled up in their blankets, between us and the window. Our escape seemed impossible; we could not slip out at the window without stepping on the soldiers; we might indeed lay still and escape detection for a while, but we knew full well that as soon as it was light enough they would load their wagon with the hay and be sure to discover us. For once I was at my wit's end.

In this predicament we lay for two long hours, when all at once we heard the alarm of fire; our good woman was calling lustily for help. In the corner of the yard about fifty feet from the house there stood a little cabin that had once been her dwelling house but which was now used as a kind of receptacle for old boxes and barrels.

This house was in flames, and we learned afterwards that she set it on fire herself to draw the soldiers from the barn so that we might effect our escape. In this she succeeded admirably; every one broke for the fire and prevented it from catching the main building, while we made our escape without any trouble whatever. We took a long breath of relief, mounted our horses and made one good night's travel. Passing near the town of Buford then west of Fredericktown, we arrived in the vicinity of Flat Woods and remained concealed in a thick forest during the day. In the evening, two of my men who were dressed in Federal uniform, wandered off from the camp and were discovered by a citizen named John Myers, who mistook them for Union soldiers and immediately commenced telling them how, thus far, he had succeeded in deceiving the Rebels. He handed them a sheet of paper on which he had written out a full report of his success in ferreting out the friends of Sam Hildebrand in that neighborhood. He stated that he was in the habit of reporting to the Rebels also, and to prove the matter he drew from his pocket a half worn paper purporting to be an account of the Federal movements in that section of country. He manifested a great desire for my capture, and when they told him that I had actually been captured and was a prisoner at their camp near by, he waved his hat and shouted like an Indian. They brought him into camp to satisfy his curiosity; but on discovering that I was not tied he started to retreat, but was stopped by my men. As soon as night began to approach we shot him and proceeded on toward Big river, but stopped in the pinery northwest from Farmington, where we remained two days. On leaving there we took supper with a friend near Big River Mills and proceeded down the river to the old Hildebrand homestead.

During Price's raid into that section of country I left word for my enemies that they should build my mother another house at the old homestead in lieu of the one they had burned, otherwise, I would burn the last one of them out. Some of my friends however, seeing that they were slow about commencing it, and wishing perhaps to screen them, met together and in a very short time built her a cabin, which answered her purpose very well for a temporary abode. Into this cabin she removed, and there I found her on the night of March 6th, 1865. I left my men and horses in a secure place near by, and quietly approached the premises where once had been the happy home of my childhood. It was late in the night when I called at the door, but my mother had not yet retired; knowing my voice she laid her spectacles upon her open bible where she had been reading, and softly opened the door. Her motherly arms entwined around my neck, the same arms that had so often lulled me to sleep in my innocent childhood, that had so often clasped me to her bosom and made me feel secure from all the dangers and storms of life. My heart beat strangely as all those dear scenes and all the events of my life in one short minute crowded through my memory. I could not help contrasting her own condition at that happy period with the cheerless present. As she took her seat I could not help noticing the calm serenity of her countenance; a quiet resignation seemed to pervade her nature. Considering the terrible loss that her kind heart had sustained in the cruel death of her three boys, and in the utter uprooting of all her cherished hopes in this world, I was at a loss to account for it, and was about to express my wonder when she seemed to divine my thoughts before my question was formed, and with a slight motion of her hand toward the bible, she said in a faltering tone: "My dear boy! you are more unhappy than I am!" The remark was so true, that I wished I had the power to obliterate the past, and to commence life again as a little frolicsome boy around my mother's chair.

I remained with her most of the time during the next day. It was her impression that the war was near its close; that the triumph of the Union cause was almost complete, and she insisted strongly that when the Southern soldiers should lay down their arms, that I with the rest would yield obedience to the government and claim its protection.

I was so softened by this interview with my mother, that I almost forgot my enemies; and I made up my mind to return to Arkansas without killing any one if I could do so with safety to myself.

But it was necessary that I and my men should take some goods with us, for our families, at this time, were rather needy; and believing that friends as well as foes should bear a part of the burden of our suffering families, inasmuch as all our energies had been directed to the accomplishment of an object which they so strenuously contended was right, we concluded to make a small raid into the town of Big River Mills that my friends might still know we were on the war path. We started late in the evening and kept along the main road, arriving in town between sundown and dark. We went to the store of J. Y. Tyler, and helped ourselves to such articles as we actually needed. After mounting our horses we did not remain long to see the balance of our friends, but hurried on all that night to get as far beyond the gravel road at night as possible.

We lay up to rest ourselves during the day; but about two o'clock in the evening, we discovered a considerable force of Federals on our track; they came to the place where our trail commenced winding around the hill, and there they began to move very cautiously.

I plainly saw from their movements that they had learned my trick of making a circuit before camping; this being the case I determined to escape by the same knowledge. We started very cautiously down the hill in an opposite direction, rode about three miles, made another circuit and went on in a great hurry. Every few miles we made a similar curve, but continued on, and by the time they had crept cautiously up to the last place we were far beyond their reach.

We had no further trouble with the Federals, and reached Arkansas with all our goods.

CHAPTER XXXIV.

Started to Missouri with three men. Surrounded at night near Fredericktown. Narrow escape by a cunning device. Retired to Simms' Mountain. Swapped horses with Robert Hill and captured some more. Killed Free Jim and kidnapped a negro boy.

About the first of April, 1865, I started to Missouri with four men, one of whom was Tom Haile. We passed west of Bloomfield, and made an attempt to take in a German living in the edge of Wayne county, whose name I never could pronounce. He had rendered himself rather obnoxious to us by his officiousness in carrying news to the Federal authorities.

On going up to his house about sunrise, thinking to find him asleep, we made no attempt at concealment, but marched directly up toward the front of his house; when we got within a hundred and fifty yards of the house he ran out and struck across a little field; we fired our guns at him, shooting one at a time; every time we fired he squalled like a panther, which tickled Tom Haile so well he could not shoot, but laughed about as loud as the Dutchman yelled. We made no attempt to pursue him, as we cared very little about him any way. We marched on toward Fredericktown, reaching that place one morning about daybreak, and secreted ourselves for the day, during which time Haile went into Fredericktown.

After tying up an old coat in a dirty cotton handkerchief, and swinging it on a stick which he carried on his shoulder, he walked into town, passing himself off for a lame Irishman who wanted a job for a few days; he found some soldiers there, but did not learn their number.

While in town he met several acquaintances who kindly passed him without recognition.

It appears, however, that in the morning as we were passing Mr. Blake's farm we were discovered by some one and reported to the soldiers.

A company was ordered out to guard a gap where we were in the habit of passing, and we distinctly heard their horses' feet on the gravel road as they passed our retreat where we lay concealed in the thick forest awaiting the approach of night.

Immediately after dark we started, but on crossing the gravel road two shots were fired at us from a short distance; we dashed through the thick brush, but my horse soon got tangled in a grapevine, and the boys all left me, vainly endeavoring to get him along.

The firing became very rapid. In riding through the thick tangled brush I made too much noise, and the first thing I knew I was completely surrounded, though their lines as yet were at some distance.

Having no time to lose I quickly dismounted, dropped the bridle rein over a snag, and ran back about one hundred yards; I stepped behind a bush and remained very quiet, knowing if I fired they would see the flash of my pistol.

They were closing up in regular order toward the point where my horse stood. I waited until they were within ten steps of me, then facing toward the horse which now gave a snort, I gave a few steps, then in a low but commanding tone, I cried out: "Advance with more caution! they can hear you a mile!" By this time I was in their line, and under the pretense of correcting some irregularity in their movements, I stepped behind them and got away without creating the least suspicion.

Being next discovered by the guard who were holding the horses, I told them that we had the bushwhackers all surrounded, and that to make a sure thing we must have more men.

Mounting the best looking horse I could find by the dim light of the moon, I started toward Fredericktown in a great hurry; but when out of danger I changed my course for Simms' mountain in St. Francois county, the place designated for our meeting in case of trouble.

The Federals probably captured my horse, but that was no loss to me, for I had obtained a much better one.

I rode all night and a part of the next day by myself before I reached our place of rendezvous. My men were not there, and as the day wore away I began to fear that some misfortune had befallen them; but they made their appearance after dark, and reported that the Federals had given them a severe chase; immediately after which they met a squad of Federals who chased them the other way.

Simms' Mountain is a very high elevation of land scarcely ever visited except by hunters at certain seasons of the year. It looms up above the other hills, affording a fine view of the whole surrounding country. While we lay here Tom Haile took a trip to Iron Mountain to learn the news at the military camp, and to get some provisions. After getting near the place he left his horse and his arms in the woods, stopped at an old coal pit to smut his face and his hands, and then went into town disguised as a collier, of whom there were many in the neighborhood. While purchasing some provisions at a store he learned that "five hundred soldiers had Sam Hildebrand surrounded in a thicket from which it was impossible for him to escape."

This was good news, for it would enable us to make a raid on Big river in broad daylight with perfect impunity. We passed down Flat river during the latter part of the night, crossed Big river at the Haile Ford and rode into town just as the sun was rising. Finding no goods there that suited us we continued along the main road until we got to the residence of our good Union friend, Robert Hill. We wished to make him a friendly visit and swap off some of our horses, for Tom Haile dissuaded me from doing him any personal injury.

I took two of his best horses and left two in their place; we charged him some boot, but had to take it in clothing and such articles from the house as we could make use of.

On leaving there we turned south and passed along the most public road four or five miles until we came to Nesbit Orton's. We took a fancy to a couple of mares that some neighbors had there, one belonging to Tom Highley and the other to Tom Crunkleton. The mare, however, which we took from the latter did not like Rebels, for on getting a few miles I concluded that she would make a splendid war horse; but she threw all my men, one at a time, and when I was about to try my luck she gave a snort, broke away from us and made her escape.

Tom Haile had remained behind to visit some of his friends on Big river, and did not overtake us until we got to Cook settlement.

I and my other men continued to travel along the road until we reached the shanty belonging to an old free negro by the name of Jim. He had made himself the dread of Southern sympathizers in his neighborhood by frequently visiting the different military posts with various charges against them, such as feeding bushwhackers, etc.

To satisfy myself in regard to his complicity in the matter, we rode up to his cabin, each one being dressed in Federal uniform.

On calling him out I gave him a hearty shake of the hand, and inquired if he had learned anything more about that man Madkins he was telling me about at the Knob; at this the old negro imagined that he recognized me as Col. — —, and asked me what I had done with my shoulder-straps; to which I replied that I wanted to find out a few things for myself, and enjoined secrecy on him in regard to my disguised appearance.

He made charges against several of the best men in the neighborhood, which was calculated to consign them to summary punishment according to Federal usage.

After making his statements, he asked me if I was still willing to take his son for a waiting boy; I told him that I was, and that I designed taking him along with me this time, having brought a horse for that purpose. He called the boy out and told him to mount the horse, which he at first refused to do; but after I had got the old negro to mount another horse for the purpose of going with us a few miles, the boy consented and seemed very well reconciled.

After going about two miles I shot old Jim, but took the boy on with us.

We stopped near the residence of Francis Clark, in Cook settlement, to get our dinners; and while there some Federals came along, but seeing us they turned off the road and went around without molesting us. We proceeded on without any further trouble, but traveled altogether in the night.

On reaching the St. Francis we found it still out of its banks; we, however, succeeded in swimming it by resting our horses on an island about half way. From there we arrived safely at home, and for the first time in my life I owned a negro. I was to all intents and purposes a genuine slaveholder.

Immediately after I left Big river on my last raid, Robert Hill became satisfied that, as I took his horses, he could no longer pass himself off for a Rebel and a Union man at the same time. He was a member both of the "Knights of the Golden Circle" and the "Union League." A few days after I "*swapped* horses" with him, he went before the provost marshal, at Potosi, and represented that in consequence of his Union sentiments he could not live at home on Big river without a band of soldiers for his protection.

Failing, however, in his purpose, he went to Ironton and made a similar statement to the provost marshal at that place. Certain Union men, however, who knew all the facts in the case, represented the whole matter as arising from personal enmity against Dr. A. W. Keith and others.

Thwarted again in his designs, he was left a few days to muse over his misfortunes; but a bright idea finally came to his relief: He would expose the "Knights of the Golden Circle," and consign his brother members to an indiscriminate butchery!

The war was nearly at an end; the Union cause was about to triumph; and one string was enough to play on during the balance of the struggle. He would startle the world by his disclosures; the earth should be dumbfounded, and mankind should stand aghast at the magnitude of his revelations! He sought and obtained a private interview with the provost marshal. At this time the sun was serenely smiling upon the earth; spring had just made her advent, and was strewing garlands of flowers along the meadows and sunny hillsides, as if nothing was about to happen; and men throughout the world, unmindful of what was about to take place, were plodding on in their daily pursuits.

All things being now ready, he told the marshal that he was a member of the Union League. This announcement was a satisfactory proof of his loyalty, for this Northern KuKlux League was instituted to save the National Union secretly.

He then stated that, for the good of his country, he had also joined the Knights of the Golden Circle; that the Circle met at the house of Joseph Herrod, on Big river, and that many of the leading men in that neighborhood were members.

The patriotic motives of Robert Hill will be very apparent to the reader, when I state that at the outbreak of the rebellion, when he joined the Golden Circle, he was a slaveholder, and utterly pro-slavery in sentiment.

How pure, then, must have been his motives when, for the good of his country, even at that early day, he bound himself with oaths like adamant for the purpose of finally exposing the Circle, as soon as it should have run its race and become defunct!

If the Southern Confederacy had won, his patriotism would have prompted him to expose the Union League; and when the last expiring beacon of Federal hope was about to be extinguished, he probably would have called for troops to crush the members of the Union League to which he belonged!

The representations he made to the provost marshal had the desired effect; a telegram was sent to Col. Beverage, at Cape Girardeau, who sent Lieutenant

Brown, with forty men, to Big River Mills.

The statement made by Hill, however, needed confirmation. It was desirable to prove the charges by some one whose word, on account of the color of his skin, could never for a moment be doubted.

A negro man by the name of Buck Poston lived in the neighborhood; his skin was black enough for him to be considered perpetually under oath, so they repaired immediately to his domicil, for the purpose of implicating certain persons as belonging to the Golden Circle.

Brown and his men put a rope around his neck, and tried to frighten him into a belief that he would be hung unless he confirmed Hill's statements. But Buck was a brave man, and answered "no" to each one of Hill's accusations against his neighbors.

Finally they told him that he was now about to be hung, and appealed to him to know if he did not love his wife and children, and urged him just to say "yes," and live; but the old man replied: "Well, Massa, I does know some little things; but I's gwine to take it all to t'other world with me!" Neither persuasions, threats, the glittering of bayonets, nor the prospect of death, could make him divulge anything.

The color of his skin, however, saved his life, and his tormentors had nothing to do but to return to camp. During the night following he gave warning to those whom he knew to be in danger.

On the next day, May 14, 1865, Lieut. Brown took four men, rode up to the house of Mr. Joseph Herrod, and found him at home. They ordered him to get his horse and go with them to Farmington. He did so, but on getting half a mile from the house, they took him twenty or thirty steps from the road and shot him through the back of the head. There they left him, where he was found the next day.

Thus perished a young man who, for kindness of heart, strict integrity, and moral honesty had no superiors, and but few equals.

Before proceeding any further with the slaughter, Lieut. Brown went and consulted with Franklin Murphy, who told him that the whole matter was the result of a neighborhood difficulty, which did not warrant Federal interference in any manner whatever.

Brown and his men, during their stay on Big river, were engaged in a wholesale robbery and plunder of the citizens, taking their property without even a promise to pay. Their depredations were even more intolerable than the same number of hostile Indians would have been; but after Brown had been better informed as to the true nature of affairs he became half civilized, and on taking property he gave government vouchers. These debts against the government, however, were finally rejected, the people having been reported as disloyal. Even the widow Baker lost over one hundred dollars by some one reporting her as a Southern sympathizer.

After feasting off of the neighborhood for about two months, Brown and his infamous band of vandals took their departure. The conspiracy, founded on the marvelous revelation of a broken oath, and emanating from the fertile brain of base malignity, suddenly collapsed.

CHAPTER XXXV.

Trip to Missouri with four men.—Attempt to rob Taylor's store.—
Fight with Lieut. Brown and his soldiers.—Killed Miller and Johnson at Flat Woods.—Return home from his last raid.—The war is
pronounced to be at an end.—Reflections on the termination of
the war.—Mrs. Hildebrand's advice.—The parole at Jacksonport.

When the war first broke out in Missouri, and after the persecutions against
the Hildebrand family had become so intolerable that I was compelled to flee the
country, I owed a small debt to D. W. Taylor, a merchant living at Valley's Mines,
in Jefferson county.

After the mob had destroyed my property and driven me into the Southern
army for protection, it was impossible for me to pay the debt during the struggle.

In all communities there are "land sharks" who are willing to befriend an
intended victim to a certain extent, but who are ready at the first approach of an
unforseen disaster to gobble up his lands.

In this instance, Taylor attached my interest in the Hildebrand homestead, and
while the country was in the ebullition of civil war, had it sold at public vendue,
bidding it in himself for a mere nominal sum.

For this little piece of ingenuity I now determined to award him with a clear
title to another small tract of land, four feet by six, to have and to hold, as his own
individual possession, until Gabriel should blow his horn.

With this intention, on the 28th day of April, 1865, I started with four men for
another raid into Missouri. We made our way quietly and cautiously through the
southern counties of Missouri, all of which were now held by Federal soldiers, for
the protection of the citizens—the *protection*, however, being the same kind that
the vulture gave the lamb.

Reaching Big river late in the night, we repaired to the Pike Run hills and slept
until morning. Knowing that we would be more apt to catch Taylor in daytime,
we started in the morning and rode over to Taylor's store, which was distant only
about six miles. He was not at home, and having no time to lose, we went into his
store and commenced selecting such goods as we wanted, when we were suddenly run on to by some Federal soldiers, under Lieut. Brown, from Perry county,
but who was at that time stationed at Big River Mills, with forty men, one-half of
whom he had with him on the present occasion.

They came up within two hundred yards of the store, and commenced firing and yelling at a terrible rate. We ran out to our horses, which were tied to the brush not more than forty yards off, but on the opposite side from the soldiers. One of my men was killed by an accidental shot, and another one who happened to be a new recruit left his horse and ran off through the woods, leaving me with an *army* of only two men, besides myself, to repel the attack of twenty regulars. The Federals, however, after their first fire, took refuge behind some old houses about one hundred and fifty yards off, and from there showed us a very harmless and cowardly fight. After I gained my horse, I used him for a fortification and shot several rounds at them; occasionally I could see one's head bob around a corner, but they were out of range, and my shots fell harmless to the ground. My other two men now left me alone, and for several minutes I remained, trying to get a dead shot at one of the Federals; but having no chance to do so, without charging them by myself, I mounted my horse and retreated, leaving my dead man upon the ground, whom they charged and shot several times after I left. I went on to an adjoining hill, but failing to find my men, I rattled my cow bell, which I had with me for emergencies of this kind, and in half an hour my three men were with me.

Having made a complete failure, it is not unreasonable to suppose that we felt very much chagrined at our ill luck, and knowing that if we started south then, we would be annoyed by Federals on our trail, we repaired again to the Pike Run hills for safety, where we could easily have whipped all the forces within the three surrounding counties. My comrade who was on foot went about four miles to the house of an old acquaintance and obtained a horse, by promising to return him again in six weeks; which promise, I will here state, he afterwards faithfully performed.

It was now about the middle of May, and we were anxious to be on our way back; so we started one night and went as far as Flat Woods.

Before McIlvaine and the soldiers had driven me from there, I became acquainted with two men, George Miller and Joseph Johnson, who professed great friendship for me; but some time after my expulsion from that neighborhood, they visited my house and used abusive language to my wife, making threats what they intended to do with me. Johnson had the impudence to remark that he intended to kill me and bring my head to her swinging to the horn of his saddle.

These were not vain threats, for they watched for me for a long time; but after they learned a little more about me, they were very shy, and up to the present time I had never got my eyes upon either of them.

Late in the evening, on the next day after our arrival in the neighborhood, as I was passing a house I saw a lady dressing some butter, and wishing for a good drink of buttermilk, I alighted a moment and went in the house. As I was dressed in Federal uniform, the good woman asked me if I was hunting for Sam Hildebrand; on telling her that I was, she went on to give me the particulars of our affray at Taylor's store, ascribing to the Federal arms the most brilliant victory, by stating that "Lieut. Brown, with only twenty men, ran upon Hildebrand's Bushwhackers and completely routed them, killing fourteen and wounding several more; a great many soldiers are now after him, and have him surrounded in a place where he can never get back here to bother us again!" I asked her if she would please give Sam Hildebrand a drink of buttermilk? She looked at me a moment and then replied: "Yes, sir; you can have all in the churn if you want it."

Not long after leaving there, I found Mr. Miller in his field, and shot him. After night I found Mr. Johnson at home, took him out of the house, and cut off his head with my bowie knife.

The reader will perceive that the threats of Johnson would have been completely reversed if I had carried his head to his wife swinging to the horn of my saddle; but instead of imitating his designs any further, I leisurely pursued my way home to our headquarters in Green county, Arkansas.

On the next day after my arrival at home, Capt. Bolin called on me and stated that he wished us all to meet him at headquarters that evening at three o'clock. At the time appointed I was there, and so were about forty more of the boys, most of whom had just returned from their various scouts.

The Captain seemed a little agitated, and for several minutes after we were all assembled he did not say a word. Presently he began, and these are about his words:

"GENTLEMEN: It is my wish that we remain quietly at head-quarters a few days until my other scouting parties return.

"I wish to say to you now that, in my opinion, this war has virtually closed. General Lee, the great head and front of all our hopes, as you are already aware, was compelled to succumb to superior numbers, and surrender on the 12th day of April. General Johnston surrendered on the 18th of the same month. The hopes held out by General Kirby Smith in his general order issued at Shreveport can never be realized.

"The Southern Confederacy is at an end; our course must be governed by circumstances over which we have no control.

"The course we have pursued during the struggle is only justified by the fact that a great war existed. While the eyes of the world have been riveted on great actors and on events of an astounding magnitude, the minor details of the struggle have been overlooked. That condition of affairs now no longer exists; the war has ceased, and our operations must cease also.

"Finally, it is my request that each and every one of you submit manfully to the same terms that have been forced upon our great chieftains; that is: Lay down your arms, surrender on parole, and return to the pursuits of peace."

This little speech fell like a wet blanket on most of the men, and I must confess that I was one of that number; but we held Capt. Bolin in such high esteem that not a murmur of dissent was suffered to drop from the lips of any of his men.

On the next day, however, the matter was fully discussed in every camp. Nine-tenths of the men fully indorsed the statements made by our noble captain, and I could not but acknowledge that his reasoning seemed plausible; yet I was annoyed beyond all measure by the reflection that the war had suddenly ceased before I was done fighting.

I cared not so much about the general result. I knew but little, and cared still less, about the great political problem that the war was supposed to have solved, nor to the technical question discussed by old fossil statesmen, whether the States formed the Union or the Union formed the States, whether the South had inherent rights or whether inherent rights had the South, whether the General Government was a restricted agent of the people, or whether the people were the restricted agents of the General Government.

These questions probably originated with the antediluvians, and they ought to have been left to a committee of twelve Egyptian mummies, with the "man in the moon" for chairman.

The practical question with me was, whether all the scoundrels in the nation were yet killed off or not. As far as my knowledge extended, the war had only gobbled up about one-tenth of them.

Most of those men who had composed the Vigilance mob on Big river were yet alive. They were in the centre of military camps, crawling around the feet of Federal officers, and whining for protection against my vengeance.

To reach them it would be necessary to overthrow the Federal power; just that far my heart was in the National war.

My mind was troubled by the reflection that as soon as the war should be ended, all those cowardly miscreants would crawl out from their hiding places, boast of their loyalty, make a grand rush for office, swing their hats, and cry out: "Well, didn't *we* whip them?"

I made up my mind that, for my part, I would take as many of the boys as were determined never to surrender, escape to Texas if possible, fight under Gen. Kirby Smith until he should surrender, and then make our way into Mexico—there to annoy the Federal Government all I could until I could get another "whack" at my old enemies.

I thought, however, that I would consult my wife for once, and see what she thought about it. She looked serious for a minute, and then burst out into a laugh.

"I once heard about some little boys," said she, "who were left at home by their parents, who had gone to church. One of them discovered a rat which had taken refuge under a pile of lumber in the yard; but the boys tore away the lumber, splitting about half the boards. The rat then ran under the ash-hopper, and when that was torn down it took refuge under the barn floor. One of the boys ran to the house for matches, in order to burn out the rat; but his little sister, the youngest one in the crowd, cried out: 'If you burn the rat we will have no barn!' The boys saw the force of her reasoning, and made peace with the rat. So I would advise you to make no further efforts toward destroying the Federal barn for such a purpose."

I must confess that this little speech from my wife, given in such good humor, contained a little more good sense than anything I had heard for a long time.

It sounded a little like a Union speech, and seemed strange on that account; but, although I had not at first the least idea of ever swerving from my purpose, yet I now determined to follow her advice, for I concluded that as she had waded through the hardships of war with a devotion to me that has but few parallels in the history of mankind, I ought to respect her comfort as well as my own.

On the next day I told Capt. Bolin that I consented to his arrangement. He started on to Jacksonport to give in the list of his men, and I started a few days afterwards to the same place, and received my parole on the 26th day of May, 1865, the very day on which General Kirby Smith surrendered at Shreveport.

The war now being over, I tried to banish the subject from my mind as much as possible, and soon went to work on the place I still occupied, for no owner had yet returned to claim it. Most of our men were afraid to return to their homes in Missouri while a remembrance of our depredations were still fresh in the minds of the people, and went to farming in different parts of Green county.

With what I captured during the war I did not have more than half as much property as I had lost by the hands of the Vigilance mob in Missouri.

One might suppose that, from the name my enemies gave me, I might have grown rich by my depredations during the war; but such was not the fact; plunder was only a secondary consideration with me; I resorted to it merely to sustain myself while I pursued my main leading object—that of killing my enemies.

We sustained ourselves during the whole war off of our enemies. If objections are made to that kind of warfare, I can point to the example of Sherman, in Georgia, and to a host of other Federal commanders, both great and small, even down to that pigmy lump of insignificance—the Big River Militia. But, unlike those illustrious examples, we did not charge our government with anything we captured; neither was I a burden to the Confederacy to the amount of one dollar; neither did I ever stoop so low as to become an incendiary, and burn out my enemies. I left that for the Indians to do, and for those who saw proper to imitate them.

So, at the close of the war, and in fact during its whole continuance, I was poor, and my family were in straitened circumstances; but I went to work and raised a good crop of corn and everything else that we needed. In the spring of 1866 I rented another place in a better locality, and farmed on a larger scale. This I also did on the year following, and at the close of 1867 I had succeeded in rendering myself and family as comfortable as could be expected.

The negro boy I had taken from Free Jim, in St. Francois county, still remained with me; he was free, I suppose, but he seemed to prefer good living and light work to "free starvation."

CHAPTER XXXVI.

Imprisoned in Jacksonport jail.—Mrs. Hildebrand returns to Missouri.—Escape from prison.—Final settlement in Ste. Genevieve county.—St. Louis detectives make their first trip.—The Governor's reward.—Wounded by Peterson.—Removed to his uncle's.—Fight at John Williams'.—Kills James McLaine.—Hides in a cave.

Early in the spring of 1868 I put in a good crop of corn, and devoted much of my time to gardening; my prospect looked flattering indeed, and I fancied that I was getting along as well as any of my neighbors, and better than most of them. My negro man worked cheerfully, and I put in much of my time in "overseeing." I claim that I was the last slaveholder in the United States.

A circumstance now took place that destroyed my future prospect, and cast a shadow over the happiness of my family. It is a circumstance that I deeply deplore, and one, too, that I you'd easily have avoided, at the expense, perhaps, of losing one friend.

Early in the month of April one of my old war associates, with whom I had passed many a hardship, came to my house and stated that he had received bad news from home; that his sister had been deserted by her husband without any cause, and that the fellow had taken up with a negro woman, and was living with her not more than ten miles off. He requested that I should aid him in taking the couple out and giving them a good flogging.

The matter was talked over, and one of us might have made the remark that they deserved to be tied together. This conversation was heard by the wife of my friend; two or three days after which the guilty pair were taken from a mill pond, drowned, and still tied together. After the first excitement was over, nothing more was heard about the matter for nearly six weeks. My friend's wife told all about the conversation, and suspicion rested upon us.

Finally Major Surge, with three men, arrested us, and took us before the authorities; the preliminary examination was had, and we were both lodged in the jail at Jacksonport.

We were secured by handcuffs and by ball and chain. In this condition it soon became apparent to us that our escape was impossible. Negroes frequently passed our prison, and told us that we would be hung by a mob.

We were loaded with chains, and so strongly guarded that I began to doubt the ability of our friends to release us, even if they should attempt it; in fact I began very strongly to doubt the probability of their ever coming at all.

In June, my brother William, who had served during the war in the Union army, came down to Arkansas, where my family was, for the purpose of taking them back to Big river, in Missouri; for the probabilities were that my wife would soon be left a widow. She sold the crop as it stood on the ground for what she could get, and hired a teamster to haul the family to Big river.

She made the trip in safety; arriving at the old homestead, she lived with my mother and brother William. My prison life every day became more intolerable. I had been in jail for four months, and had almost abandoned all hopes of being released.

On the last day of August, as I lay brooding over my helpless condition, some one, about dark, whispered in through the grates, telling me to be of good cheer, for that on the following night his friends were going to make an attempt to release me.

Fortunately for us, as our friends lay in wait on the next night, a boat landed at the wharf, which attracted the attention of all those who were yet up, and we were let out without any disturbance whatever.

I was so overjoyed at the idea of being free once more, that I leaped off the platform in the dark and sprained my ankle. I was in a bad fix for traveling, but we were soon out of danger. I rode until daylight; then we all scattered, and each one took his own course. I hobbled on in this way, living on nothing but May-apples until I made about thirty-five miles, to the house of an old friend, where I remained until I recruited up, and then I started to where my family was, in Missouri. I found them at my mother's residence, on Big river; but after remaining a few weeks, finding that my presence was anything but pleasing to my old enemies I removed to Illinois and settled on the Mississippi, about forty miles below St. Louis. Here I went to chopping cord wood for a livelihood, not intending to molest any one, as the war was over, and fully determined to withhold my hand from the commission of any act that would indicate anything else than that I was a peaceable and law-abiding citizen.

In January, 1869, I moved across the river on to the Missouri side, at a place called Rush Tower, and continued cutting wood until the first of April, at which time I rented a small farm of Samuel B. Herrod, on the Three Rivers, in Ste. Genevieve county, near the county line of St. Francois, and about four miles from Big River Mills. To this place I moved my family. My oldest boy was twelve years old, and on him devolved most of the labor on the farm.

My arrival seemed to create a panic among those who had robbed me, killed my brothers, and persecuted my family. They still had a fear of retributive justice, and though I had no such designs, they secretly went to work to effect my destruction.

Joe McGahan, as I am informed, took several trips to influence the Governor of Missouri to crush me out of existence. Gov. McClurg instructed Col. Myers, Police Commissioner of St. Louis, to send out men for my arrest. In May, 1869, he sent McQueen and Col. Bowen, who were met at Irondale by Joe McGahan, to pilot them to the scene of operations. On going about ten miles, however, daylight overtook them, and McGahan, after informing them that to be seen there in daylight would be death to him, went on home and never returned. At the approach of night the detectives were obliged to proceed without a guide, on foot, and in a strange neighborhood. After wandering around all night, wading Big river at a deep ford, they were obliged to pass another day in the woods. As they could not find my house without some further information, one of them, disguised as a rude country man in search of employment, got all the information he wanted. It appears that those two detectives watched around my house for eight days and nights. Their provisions then gave out, and not being able to get any from my enemies, they started back to Irondale at ten o'clock at night, and from there took the cars for St. Louis. While this was going on I was working at the mouth of Isle Bois on the Mississippi.

It appears that some time during the war Governor Fletcher had offered a reward of three hundred dollars for my capture.

This and other rewards which were offered was the price of blood — an inducement held out for assassination! Men can be found, who, for a certain reward, will shoot any man down whom a Governor may designate.

Thank God, I have never come to that yet! I have killed many men, but it has always been either in self-defense, or for the purpose of redressing some terrible wrong.

Some persons wrote to Governor McClurg to ascertain whether the reward was still valid; on being answered in the affirmative, they determined, even for that paltry sum, to attempt my assassination. James McLaine, as he afterwards boasted, prowled around my house for one whole month for that purpose.

On the night of June 6th, 1869, I ventured up to my house at a late hour to see my family, and remained with them all night. In the morning I stepped out into the yard, when I heard the report of a gun from a cluster of hazel brush about eighty yards off. I went into the house for my gun, and discovered that I had been shot through the fleshy part of my thigh.

On going out I could discover no one, the person having left as soon as he fired, so I went into Mr. Pratt's stable, a short distance off. Presently McLaine passed by with his gun; after going up to my house, he came back and passed along the road not far from the stable. Believing him to be the assassin, I would have shot him, but was prevented by Mr. Pratt.

I was hauled to the house of William M. Highley, who went after a physician to have my wound dressed. The wound proved to be a very serious one, and disabled me for a long time in such a manner that I was unable to walk. I was next hauled to Samuel Gossom's, and then to the residence of my uncle, John Williams. As this became the scene of a furious battle a few days afterwards, I shall be a little minute in my description. My uncle's family consisted of himself, Aunt Mary and a granddaughter about six years of age. His house is among the hills in the western part of St. Francois county, five miles from Big River Mills, and one mile due south from the stone house formerly occupied by Dick Berryman. My uncle's premises consisted of one log house, one story high, and containing but one room. In the yard west of the house stood an old dilapidated cabin with the chimney torn down, near which stood the smoke-house and a cluster of young cherry trees. Opposite the south end of the house, at a distance of about eighty yards, was the spring house.

I suffered much from my wound; and as my well known crippled condition emboldened parties afterwards to attempt my arrest, under the assumption that I was just about dead, I attribute all my sufferings and privations during the three months that followed to that attempted assassination. For many months afterwards I believed that it was James McLaine who did the deed, but I will here state that the man who shot me, as I am informed, was Cyrus A. Peterson, from Fredericktown, and that Walter E. Evans was along with him.

Neither of those two men did I ever harm; Peterson I did not know, and Evans I had met a few weeks before, and shook hands with him.

The Evans family resided on Big river, and we were raised up within a few miles of each other. The widow and her daughter remained at home in perfect safety during the whole war, although the family was known to be Union (with one or two exceptions), and two of her boys, Ellis G. and William C. Evans, were known to be two of the most uncompromising Unionists in the State. I heard Dick Berryman once tell his men, after calling them all up in a line, that he would not suffer them to interfere with the widow Evans, or with any property that she possessed. This order I sanctioned, and governed myself accordingly.

While I still lay at my uncle's, confined to my bed, Sheriff Breckinridge and a party of about six men concluded that they would secure the reward offered by the Governor without any personal danger, as it was thought by some that I had died of my wounds.

During the night he went with his party to Mr. Highley's, and got near the house by keeping behind a gate-post. Mr. Highley was called out, and when he assured them that I was not there they made a valiant charge upon the house, and entered it just as Mrs. Highley was endeavoring to put on her dress. The gallant Breckinridge thrust his gun against her dress and threw it to the other side of the room, denoting thereby that cowardice and ruffianism are blended together. From here they went on the balance of the night in search of "Sam Hildebrand"—*and they found him*!

They reached Uncle William's about daylight. Finding him at the crib they made a breastwork of him, by making the old man walk in front, while they marched on behind with their guns presented. I fastened the front door and refused to open it. The back door, however, was only latched, and a child could have opened it. I pulled a little rag out of a crack near the jamb, and as they attempted to pass I fired four shots at them before they fired at all; one tumbled up behind the ash-hopper, and the others dashed back around the corner to the front side of the house. They fired several shots through the door, which struck the wall at the back of the house a few inches over the bed where the little girl lay. She raised a terrible yell; Aunt Mary ran to her, supposing that she had been shot. "Come away with her," said I, "and both of you stand in yon corner; break her a piece of pie to stop her crying, so that I can hear what is going on." I got two more shots through the crack near the chimney, one of which was at Noah Williams; he got in the chimney corner, and was hunting for a crack, but I found it first, and sent a shot after him that raked across his breast, and tore his clothes in such a manner that he left in disgust. They kept firing through the door; the beds were literally riddled; aunt got a shot on her chin; a whole volley was now fired through the door; one little shot struck her on the head, and five holes were shot through her dress.

They now marched the old man in front of them to the door; he stood with his right hand against the door-facing, and cried out: "Sam, open the door or they will kill me!"

"Hold on, Uncle," I replied, "and step out of the way."

Just then I opened the door, and crossing my arms I fired to the right and left with my pistols. Uncle's hand being in the way, I could only shoot Breckinridge through the groin, and another man through the shoulder.

Andy Bean broke to run, and jumped the fence by a walnut tree just as a shot passed through his fiery red whiskers, grazing his face sufficiently to saturate them, and to make him believe that they were one huge stream of blood. The whole party now broke, and on leaping the fence fired off their guns, some of their shots piercing the door, one passed through my uncle's wrist, some struck the house, and some missed creation.

The man wounded in the shoulder was taken to the spring to have water poured on his wound, Breckinridge to Frank Simms to have his life written, and Andy Bean to Irondale to have the arteries of his whiskers taken up. Aunt Mary now brought me a bucket of water and left, after telling me that there were provisions enough in the house to last a week.

Telegraphic dispatches were sent to St. Louis, Potosi and Farmington for more men. James McLaine and Dennis O'Leary came from Farmington, and Captain Todd Hunter with eight or ten men came from Potosi and Irondale, and, from a hill two hundred yards off, kept up an occasional fire at the house during the balance of the day. The party behind the spring house were compelled to remain there on account of my shots; they, however, kept up a random fire, to show to their anxious companions that they were not yet dead. They once held a hat around the corner of the spring house, and instantly got a hole shot through it.

While the firing still continued, I tried my hand at cooking my dinner. After eating a hearty meal and resting myself a little, I went on duty again.

About sunset McLaine climbed upon the old cabin near the house, but as there were three walls between us, the cracks did not range right for me to shoot him. After he had kindled a fire on the roof he came down and stood near the door on the far side of the cabin. I got a glimpse of his body, and by a lucky chance I shot him dead.

This created such an excitement that, as they crowded around his body, which they carried a short distance, I opened the back door, and unperceived by any of them, crawled out through the weeds and through the fence. Here I had to leave my gun, as I could not carry it, for I could not walk a step on account of my wounded leg. I crawled through the woods about two miles, for darkness now favored my escape, and arriving at the house of a friend, I obtained a horse and rode to my sister's (Mrs. Adams), living near the old homestead of the Hildebrand family.

It was necessary that I should keep in a cool place on account of my wound, so I went into my cave in the Big river bluff, half a mile north from the residence of G. W. Murphy, and near the Pike Run hills, where I remained some time, my provisions being brought to me every day by my sister. My wife and children still remained on the Herrod place, where they were watched so closely that they could not come to my assistance.

SAM HILDEBRAND'S LAST BATTLE.

CHAPTER XXXVII.

Military operations for his capture.—Col. Bowen captures the Cave.—Progress of the campaign.—Advent of Gov. McClurg.—The militia called out.—Don Quixote affair at the Brick Church.—The campaign ended.—Mrs. Hildebrand escapes to Illinois.—"Sam" leaves Missouri.—His final proclamation.

My narrative would not be complete without a history of the military operations carried on by authority of the State government for my capture or destruction; yet I must depend almost exclusively upon what my friends told me from time to time as those events were transpiring.

A few days after the fight at Williams', a detective with a dirty face and hair uncombed; riding an old mule, with a pack saddle and blind bridle, went to Big River Mills, and inquired of Dr. Keith and Samuel B. Herrod where "Sam Hildebrand" was, as he was an old "war chum" whom he wanted to assist. His ragged coat and old hat condemned him at once as a detective, for we were in the habit of dressing well during the war, as our *credit* was always good while we were well armed. He failed to elicit any information from them; in fact at this time I was nursing my wounds in the cave, and the dismal scene of my suffering was only visited by that angel of mercy, a kind sister.

It appears that the Police Commissioner of St. Louis sent Col. Bowen, McQueen, Schuster and Wadkins on a second expedition against me. They were joined at Irondale by Hughes, King, Fatchet and Zoleman; and on Big river by Joe McGahan and Dennis O'Leary.

Col. Bowen, with his men, went to the house of my sister on the 21st day of June, just before daylight, and questioned her about where I was. My sister of course refused to answer any of their questions, but on threatening to hang two of her youngest boys, one of them divulged all that he knew.

On the evening of the 22d the party arrested William Harris, my brother-in-law, also Mr. Cash and Mr. Dunham, and hung them up by the neck until they extorted from them the fact that I lived in a cave in a certain bluff which they described. This bluff rises perpendicularly nearly three hundred feet above the waters of Big river, which runs at its base. A skirt of high timber on the margin of the river in a great measure hides the bold front of this towering mass of rock from view.

The cave can be seen neither from the top nor bottom, for it is about two hundred feet from the bottom, and is hid by a projecting rock in front. From the cave in one direction along the seam in the rock there is a narrow and very difficult causeway running several hundred yards where it can be approached from above and below. This narrow turnpike can easily be defended by one man against five hundred. I regret that I was not in my castle when Col. Bowen and his posse were prowling around in front of the cave on the morning of the 23d, I would have had more fun than I did at Williams' house, where they had so much the advantage of me.

I retired from the cave during the night, and was absent when the party came to see my castle. They remained near the cave all day, but did not think it prudent to peep in to see whether I was at home or not. On the following night they built a large fire on the projection in front of the cavern, and kept it supplied with wood which they threw from the top of the bluff.

On the next morning they learned from Mr. Nash, whom they hung by the neck awhile, that I was not in the cave.

On receiving this welcome information the party scaled the bluff and took the whole place by storm. The next move to capture me was through a confession made by a son of Mr. Nash, that he was to meet me at a certain point at night with a quart of whisky.

Col. Bowen determined to capture me and the "*quart,*" so he and his party reconnoitered the place for several hours, but I kept two hundreds yards from them. They were welcome to the whisky, for I considered it my treat; and after taking a hearty drink from the branch I went away perfectly satisfied.

After the capture of my cave, Col. Bowen made his headquarters at G. W. Murphy's. There of course he lived well; the boys were all happy, drawing good wages and incurring no danger, for I solemnly promised my friends that I would not kill a single one of them unless they should indeed discover me. The first time I saw Col. Bowen after his removal to Murphy's was three or four days after he had captured the bluff. I was aiming to cross the road two or three hundred yards east of Murphy's house, when on getting in a small glade fifteen steps from the road I heard horses' feet coming from the direction of Big River Mills. I stood behind a cedar bush with a cocked pistol in each hand. Col. Bowen rode by me with two of his men, but none of them turned their heads, and I moved around the bush as they passed.

I did not wish to hurt them; I had a high regard for the Colonel, and respected him for his magnanimity in not burning my cave after he had captured it, for I must say that he was the first man who ever drove me out of a place without setting it on fire.

A few days after this I concluded to hobble over to where my family was, for the purpose of paying them a short visit; but on passing through a wheat field I was discovered by a certain man who reported me. Col. Bowen took a squad of men to watch around my house at night. Before arriving there it was dark and raining; and as I heard the tramp of their horses I stepped out of the road until they had passed. I followed them on until they got near the house and commenced placing out their pickets.

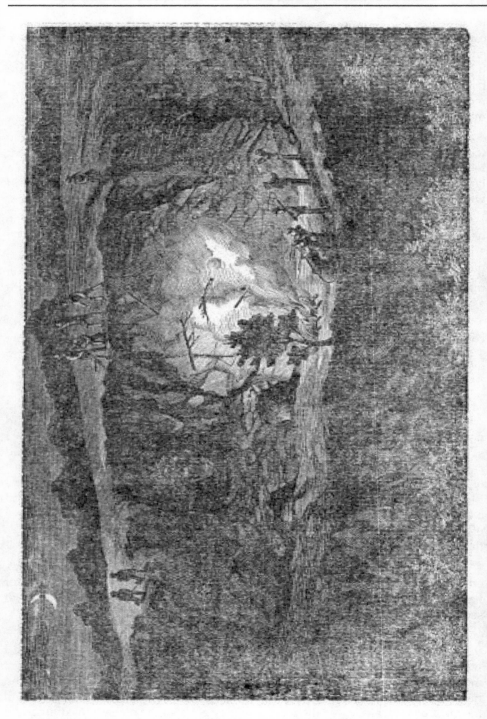

COL. BOWEN CAPTURES HILDEBRAND'S CAVE.

After the campaign had continued several weeks, it became apparent that the forces already in the field were insufficient for my capture; the disloyalty of the people of St. Francois county had been greatly magnified. Certain evil men in the neighborhood desired nothing so much as a pretext for martial law; some of them had rioted in murder and pillage during the war, and they knew that in all civil commotions the dregs arise to the top.

Governor McClurg is a good man; I can say that much for him, but in the goodness of his nature he is slow in detecting the evil designs of some of his party friends who live in the under current of cunning rascality. To show the tardiness and disloyalty of the civil authorities in St. Francois county, Sheriff Murphy was ordered, just as the farmers had whetted their scythes and were preparing to enter their harvest fields, to call out the militia throughout the county to aid in scouring the woods. To the mortification of the plotters, he responded and the people turned out.

Then the report was started that I was concealed in a deep mineral shaft among the Pike Run Hills. Murphy and his party scrambled over that terrible country until every snake was crushed by their feet.

This severe ordeal continued for two or three weeks until fortunately the Governor made his advent on Big river, and was welcomely received by all parties. To my regret I was out of the ring; however, I was anxious to see Governor McClurg, for I had never yet seen a Governor; and having been informed by my friends that he would make a speech in Farmington on the following day, I posted myself in the corner of a fence at the end of a lane on the Green place about five miles from Farmington and watched for him to come along, knowing that he would pass on that road.

I did not intend to molest him, or even to speak an unkind word; but I was anxious that he might be alone so that I could step out, shake him by the hand, give him a drink out of my bottle, and have a social chat.

When he passed me he was riding by the side of a Methodist preacher from Caledonia, named Williams; he was followed by a train of about forty men, the saints being in front and the sinners in the rear. Not liking the rear-guard very well, I did not join in the procession, but retired further back in the woods.

Under the impression that the Governor would deliver a speech at the court house that night, I concluded that I would go and hear what he had to say about me. After dark I made my way to town and secreted myself opposite the court house door among some goods boxes near Fleming's store.

I saw no indications, however, of a public meeting; I made a motion to adjourn, which was seconded by a large woolly dog that found me occupying his sleeping apartment.

I ascertained afterwards that McClurg did make a speech during the day, and that it was anything but flattering to me. To avoid the necessity of a resort to martial law, the citizens were very clamorous in their protestations of holy horror at the very name of Hildebrand. They passed a long string of resolutions; the first declaring that "Sam Hilderbrand ought to be arrested;" the second that "it would be proper to arrest Sam Hilderbrand;" the third "that to arrest Sam Hilderbrand would be a good idea;" the other sixteen resolutions not differing materially from the first three, I need not repeat.

The resolutions being read to me a few days afterwards, I fully sanctioned them, and cruised around several days myself, in search of desperadoes.

Governor McClurg appointed six deputy sheriffs for St. Francois county; their number was afterwards increased to ten, each one of whom were allowed a posse of ten men, by which arrangement one hundred men would be in active service.

In order to create the impression that he was performing some prodigious deeds of valor, Col. Bowen pretended to have fought a terrible battle single handed with "Sam Hildebrand and his men" at the Brick Church on Big river.

I have heard the battle at the Brick Church frequently mentioned, and I have a word to say in regard to that matter. I was not there myself, neither was any of my friends at the time the firing took place.

The whole tragedy was concocted by the cunning of Col. Bowen himself, in order to cut a figure and stamp himself a hero.

I could easily have killed him at any time previous to this, but as he had done me no harm, and was not likely to do any, I took the advice of my friends and let him peaceably pursue his brilliant campaigns for the sake of eclipsing the renown of Don Quixote.

It seems that two of his men had stationed themselves in the brush near the Brick Church by the road leading from his headquarters at G. W. Murphy's to Big River Mills. On a certain evening between sunset and dark, when Sheriff Murphy and himself were riding by the church on their way from Big River Mills, those two men in ambush fired off their guns. The valiant Colonel drew out his pistol and commenced firing; but to prevent the sheriff from taking a pop at the two men, he cried out to him to dash on to Big River Mills for more men, which he did and soon returned.

The Colonel remained on the ground and was master of the field, but his horse was slightly wounded by a shot nearly perpendicular, which might have been made by himself. The horse, however, not understanding the matter thoroughly, threw his master high in the air; but luckily the Colonel came down head foremost, and striking on a rock he received no injury except a ringing in his head like the rattling of a cow-bell.

He dispatched one of his men to Irondale to telegraph to the authorities at St. Louis the astounding intelligence that at the Brick Church, Col. Bowen had encountered the irrepressible "Sam Hildebrand" and his band of out-laws; that his horse had been shot from under him, but that single-handed he had driven the enemy from the field, and only received a slight wound. This Don Quixote campaign against me terminated in a spree, and the Colonel returned to St. Louis.

Previous to this, however, by Col. Bowen's orders, my wife and children were removed, first to Irondale and then to Farmington; they remained at the latter place under the supervision of the sheriff for a month. They were kindly treated, but my wife was anxious to escape from the ceaseless annoyance of Bowen's military operations.

On a certain night a friend of mine from Illinois, named Crittenden, proceeded into Farmington with a light wagon, and before the break of day my wife and family were in Ste. Genevieve county, on their way to Illinois. They stopped for breakfast at a house by the roadside, and by a strange coincidence it proved to be the house of the late James McLaine. The widow, not knowing the party, made them very welcome, and in apologizing for her straitened circumstances, observed: "I am now left a destitute widow, and all these poor little children of mine are left orphans, by the hand of Sam Hildebrand."

Mrs. McLaine's father, George Shumate was present, and while the good woman was preparing breakfast, he addressed himself to Crittenden, and gave a terrible account of my desperate deeds.

After breakfast the party arose to continue their journey; the widow would have nothing for her trouble. My wife, taking Mrs. McLaine kindly by the hand, said:

"Mrs. McLaine, I am sorry for you—truly sorry for you and your dear little children; sorry for the many hardships you have had to encounter. I know how to sympathize with you, for I am a widow myself."

"You a widow?"

"Yes, Mrs. McLaine; I am worse than a widow—I am the wife of Sam Hildebrand!"

The good woman stood amazed and said nothing; but the look that Mr. Shumate gave Crittenden was truly comical: he drew up his neck, threw his head a little back, and exclaimed:

"Well—my—God! and you are not Sam Hildebrand—are you?"

"Oh, no sir! I am not; but his wife here is my cousin."

They continued on to Illinois, and as soon as all military operations against me in Missouri had subsided, I left the State; and since that time I have been wandering through the Southern States as a peaceable citizen.

The Governor's reward against me, of course, is still unrepealed; and I hope that it will be chiseled into one of the pillars of the State Capitol, that it may be handed down to posterity in the same category with two rewards offered during the last generation—one for a feasible northwest passage, and the other for the invention of perpetual motion.

Let the legend pass down the corridors of time to the latest generation, that the strange flickering light sometimes seen at night in the dreary lowlands of the South is none other than "Jack with his lantern" trying to get the reward by finding Sam Hildebrand.

If the strange hallucination should ever enter the mind of a man that I could be captured, let him immediately send for a physician, have his head emptied and filled up with clabber to give him a better set of brains.

All fighting between "Uncle Sam" and myself has ceased long ago. He came out of the war unconquered—and so did I.

It will be a long time, however, before he gets entirely over the effects of our fight. I am hale, and have the free use of my limbs; but his southern arm is paralyzed, he is terribly in debt, can only see out of one eye, and his constitution is broken; he has the KuKlux nightmare, the Salt Lake cancer; the African leprosy, the Fenian rickets, the bondholder's cramp, and the Congressional blind staggers. The war left me out of debt, with a good horse, and forty dollars in cash.

As several proclamations have been issued against me, without ever eliciting one in return, I shall now swing my hat and proclaim:

"Peace and good will to all men; a general amnesty toward the United States, and to 'Uncle Sam'—so long as the said Uncle Sam shall behave himself."

Lector House believes that a society develops through a two-fold approach of continuous learning and adaptation, which is derived from the study of classic literary works spread across the historic timeline of literature records. Therefore, we aim at reviving, repairing and redeveloping all those inaccessible or damaged but historically as well as culturally important literature across subjects so that the future generations may have an opportunity to study and learn from past works to embark upon a journey of creating a better future.

This book is a result of an effort made by Lector House towards making a contribution to the preservation and repair of original ancient works which might hold historical significance to the approach of continuous learning across subjects.

HAPPY READING & LEARNING!

LECTOR HOUSE LLP
E-MAIL: lectorpublishing@gmail.com

9 789390 215362

www.ingramcontent.com/pod-product-compliance
Lightning Source LLC
LaVergne TN
LVHW091054090525
810824LV00023B/61